EASY TAROT
COMBINATIONS

EASY TAROT
COMBINATIONS

HOW TO CONNECT THE CARDS
FOR INSIGHTFUL READINGS

JOSEPHINE ELLERSHAW

Llewellyn Publications • Woodbury, Minnesota

First Edition
Second Printing, 2023

Book design by Mandie Brasington
Cover design by Shannon McKuhen
Editing by Laura Kurtz
Interior card spreads by Llewellyn Art Department
Tarot Original 1909 Deck © 2021 with art created by Pamela Colman Smith and Arthur
    Edward Waite. Used with permission of LoScarabeo.

Llewellyn Publications is a registered trademark of Llewellyn Worldwide Ltd.

Library of Congress Cataloging-in-Publication Data (Pending)
ISBN: 978-0-7387-7271-4

Llewellyn Worldwide Ltd. does not participate in, endorse, or have any authority or responsibility concerning private business transactions between our authors and the public.

All mail addressed to the author is forwardsed but the publisher cannot, unless specifically instructed by the author, give out an address or phone number.

Any internet references contained in this work are current at publication time, but the publisher cannot guarantee that a specific location will continue to be maintained. Please refer to the publisher's website for links to authors' websites and other sources.

Llewellyn Publications
A Division of Llewellyn Worldwide Ltd.
2143 Wooddale Drive
Woodbury, MN 55125-2989
www.llewellyn.com

Printed in the United States of America

Other Books by Josephine Ellershaw

Easy Tarot: Learn to Reads the Cards Once and For All! (2007)

Easy Tarot Reading: The Process Revealed in Ten True Readings (2011)

The Chronicles of Destiny Fortune Cards (2014, Schiffer Publishing)

About the Author

For Josephine Ellershaw, the tarot has been a constant life companion on a personal journey that now spans five decades. She is the author of the international bestseller *Easy Tarot: Learn to Read the Cards Once and For All*, along with other titles: *Easy Tarot Reading* and *The Chronicles of Destiny Fortune Cards*. Based in North Yorkshire, England, Josie provides professional readings and mentoring to an international clientele.

*In memory of Hamsavatar Das,
my Vedic astrologer and spiritual guide of many years,
who departed this realm whilst I was finishing this book.
Sincere gratitude for your guidance, friendship,
unwavering support, and encouragement to stand
up and follow my dharma.*

Acknowledgments

From an author's perspective, writing can be an intense but solitary process, yet there's a whole army of people who quietly occupy an unseen universe in the publishing house standing beside you. Behind the scenes they magically transform a manuscript into the finished item of "The Book," until it finally lands in its shiny new cover.

To all the team at Llewellyn, who play such a huge role in the ongoing process before, during, and after we go to print, my sincere thanks and appreciation for everything you have done, and continue to do, in relation to my books.

With special thanks to my editor, Barbara Moore, for your wisdom and experience, support, and encouragement; your emails always arrive with smiles and sparkles to brighten the day. To my eagle-eyed production editor, Laura Kurtz, as we navigated some of the quirky differences between English and American language; I'm in awe of your skill and patience—and the fact you can do this every day!

Over the course of the last ten years, I've had the great pleasure to work with around a thousand students on an individual basis, and this book wouldn't have been written had it not been for their persistent requests. I regret there are too many of you to personally mention, but I value the time we shared together and the insights you afforded me. I'm sorry it took me so long but hope it contains all you asked for.

As tarot readers, our clients arrive seeking guidance and answers, but through the experience we also gain knowledge through this mystical energy exchange as they sit across our table and open their lives and secrets to us. The information featured here is a result of all they taught and continue to teach me, and I'm grateful to those who entrust me with their confidences.

Sincere thanks to my family for their ongoing support and understanding when I was totally submerged in writing and missing in action—Daph, Rob and Hannah, Ems and Dave, and our little munchkins, you're the best!

Special mention to Judy, Jennifer, and Gary, for your optimism and much needed light relief at just the right moment when I was buried in words and needed to come up for air.

With gratitude to my readers, without whom none of this would be possible; thank you for your continued support!

Contents

Introduction **1**

Chapter One: Overview

What Are Tarot Combinations?   5

Building the Picture   6

How to Read a Tarot Combination   6

How to Use This Book and What's
Inside   11

Making Friends with Your Deck   15

**Chapter Two: The Minor Arcana: Applied
Meanings and Combinations**

Ace of Wands   19

Two of Wands   23

Three of Wands   27

Four of Wands   30

Five of Wands   33

Six of Wands   36

Seven of Wands   39

Eight of Wands   42

Nine of Wands   45

Ten of Wands   48

Page of Wands   51

Knight of Wands   54

Queen of Wands   57

King of Wands   60

Ace of Cups   63

Two of Cups   67

Three of Cups   70

Four of Cups   73

Five of Cups   76

Six of Cups   79

Seven of Cups   82

Eight of Cups   85

Nine of Cups   88

Ten of Cups   91

Page of Cups   94

Knight of Cups   97

Queen of Cups   100

King of Cups   103

Ace of Swords   106

Two of Swords   109

Three of Swords   113

Four of Swords   116

Five of Swords   119

Six of Swords   123

Seven of Swords   126

Eight of Swords   129

Nine of Swords   132

Ten of Swords   135

Page of Swords   138

Knight of Swords   141

Queen of Swords   144

King of Swords   147

Ace of Pentacles   150

Two of Pentacles   153

Three of Pentacles   156

Four of Pentacles   159

Five of Pentacles   162

Six of Pentacles   165

Seven of Pentacles   168

Eight of Pentacles   171

Nine of Pentacles   174

Ten of Pentacles   177

Page of Pentacles   180

Knight of Pentacles   183

Queen of Pentacles   186

King of Pentacles   189

Chapter Three: The Major Arcana: Applied Meanings and Combinations

0–The Fool   195

I–The Magician   198

II–The High Priestess   202

III–The Empress   206

IV–The Emperor   210

V–The Hierophant   214

VI–The Lovers   218

VII–The Chariot   223

VIII–Strength   227

IX–The Hermit   230

X–Wheel of Fortune   233

XI–Justice   236

XII–The Hanged Man   240

XIII–Death   244

XIV–Temperance   247

XV–The Devil   251

XVI–The Tower   255

XVII–The Star   259

XVIII–The Moon   262

XIX–The Sun   266

XX–Judgement   270

XXI–The World   273

Chapter Four: Final Notes

The Probable Future   279

Six Degrees of Separation   280

Breaking It Down:
Reading Checklist Summary   280

Endnote   283

Bibliography   285

Introduction

The many facets of tarot never fail to amaze and inspire us with the different and varying ways the cards can be used, from providing personal insights to helpful guidance when reading for others. Yet of all the questions that arise regarding tarot reading, the one I'm most consistently asked is how to link the cards to tell the story they're trying to convey. Once the individual cards are known, trying to join them together to produce a cohesive reading can be where some people start to feel discouraged. If you've ever felt this way, I'd like to reassure you that there's no need, and it's a perfectly normal part of the process until you find your feet. You may even be heartened to hear that those disjointed cards could actually form a certain type of combination too! In tarot, everything means something, even if at first it may not seem immediately apparent.

The way in which you read your cards is as unique and individual as you are; as you progress, you'll start to add your own interpretation and flavour gained through your own tarot journey and reading experiences over time. To begin, most people usually follow someone else's methods or a particular tradition and school of thought, adapting and adopting various styles until they feel comfortable and confident enough to branch out in their own way.

For the purposes of this book, we need to be sharing the same thought process in order for things to make sense, so what I share here is my own way of reading cards, developed over some fifty years. If my style is slightly different from yours, I can only encourage you to explore and experiment with an open mind to see if the results work for you and then adapt as necessary to suit your own purpose.

Similarly, some of my interpretations may vary from yours, but you can make adjustments if or when you choose. To begin, we both need to be speaking the same language, so please consider it a starting point or guidepost on your journey. As with all readers, your methods and interpretations will naturally evolve through time and experience. This book is intended to help guide you through those next steps into reading what are more commonly referred to as tarot combinations.

I

Overview

What Are Tarot Combinations?

In simple terms, tarot combinations are created once we have more than one card in a spread; the way they merge and blend together as we read from one to the next produces a combined meaning. In addition to the story the cards weave together when side by side, they can also add depth and a further dimension to your reading through their relationship or reinforcement of one another, and there are certain cards that, when appearing either as a sequence or collectively, provide some notable and special connections. Tarot reading is made up of a series of layers and connecting patterns, and card combinations fall within that framework.

In the early stages of working with your cards, you probably learnt to look for a suit that dominated the reading to show the main influence—in doing so, you were already starting to recognise one form of combination. But there are other levels available to you once you know how to apply them and where to look; we'll cover some of them as we progress. Once you understand the principles, I hope you'll discover that combinations aren't like lists that you need to memorise—although some may become fixtures in your reading toolbox—but rather an extension to the way you read your cards.

Building the Picture

Have you ever watched an artist create a painting from a blank canvas? It's quite a mesmerising process: they place the initial brushstrokes and gradually build up layers of colour, defining and blending with contrast and tone as the image starts to emerge until the final touches reveal the finished painting. Reading tarot is not too dissimilar; we start to build the story from the images cast before us. We have multiple tools at our disposal but don't always have to use everything available to uncover the hidden information, which at times can reveal itself more easily than at others. We are the seers; the skill and art of our craft means we apply our insight and knowledge to see beyond the one-dimensional through various connections of patterns and themes we find in the cards.

The spreads we use are like networks of portals, gateways that hold information that communicate messages from the cards and where you make those connections. Like opening a door and looking into an aspect of the client's life, the card meanings inform you of what lies inside. Following the pathways shows where things are heading, one situation flowing and melding into the next. Each spread or layout provides a different purpose or function depending upon what information you need at the time, though tarot combinations can be applied no matter which you choose. Most readers develop reliable and trusted favourites, but it doesn't need to be complicated—even the simple line method can provide what you need.

How to Read a Tarot Combination

Most people are familiar with and have used three-card readings (usually past, present, future), so working your way through a well-shuffled deck by reading pairs or triplets taken straight from the top can be an effective way to practice. Saying one or two keywords as you lay down each card creates an initial outline that's useful for when you go back to expand upon the interpretations further. Once you've covered the card meanings, you can look for other shared associations, such as elements or multiple numbers, to provide additional insight and depth.

The majority of the featured combinations show a simple timeline working from left to right, so the intention we're setting is that we always read forwards in time and never back over ourselves, as it can change the interpretation. It sounds simple, but it can catch you off guard if you're working with a large amount of cards, as there can be a tendency to leapfrog ahead.

In a simple line, each event or action in a card leads to the next one occurring or in some way bringing about the circumstances found in the following card, creating a domino effect. In this way, we have a string of events all connected and starting from the first card, with the final card as the most likely outcome of the situation, at least within a given timeframe. For example:

[Current issue/background] > [Leads to this event unfolding next] > [Results in this potential outcome].

When using a positional spread that has set titles for each placement to help provide context, combinations can still apply: look at the cards collectively as an overall picture rather than viewing each set position completely independently. In effect, we could say we have three ways of working with combinations:

- Cards linked together that form a series of events happening one after another.
- Cards that blend together smoothly and read like a sentence to indicate one particular event.
- A group of cards appearing anywhere in the spread when taken collectively that highlight a shared meaning and provide another layer to your reading.

Four-Card Formation

The addition of a fourth card to your usual three can be helpful, especially in general readings because we can use it as the "root" card—the main theme or influence, or what this is all about, to provide a starting point. The circumstances described by this card should already be exerting its influence and, if not, suggests it is imminent.

For example:

Shuffle and cut the cards in your usual way, say your keywords to yourself as you lay down each card taken sequentially from the top of the deck, and then expand your interpretation.

- The root card and main theme at the moment
- What it's all about or how it began
- Will in some way be connected and lead to events in Card 2

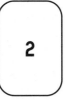

- Events from Card 1 brought this into being
- May already be happening or just about to
- Leads to Card 3

- As the situation unfolds, this is what will happen next in the progression and chain of events
- Leads to Card 4

- Closes the sequence of where events lead in this situation—as far in time as we can foresee at the moment

One of the things we always like to see is a difficult situation improving as each card unfolds into the next, rather than the other way round; when you find difficult cards, you don't want to see them gathering steam or gaining momentum. You can have three negative cards in a row yet end with a positive card that, being the last card, has the final say as the outcome or situation to which the other cards will lead. It can also work the other way round; you're often holding your breath until the last card goes down!

Another formation to watch for is what I call a trapped card, where a positive card is surrounded by or with negative cards to either side which is usually termed as "badly aspected." Although it may not necessarily change the card meaning (which should still be experienced), it hems in the positive energy and prevents it from exerting its full influence to its best advantage since the end result is a negative card. For this reason, I sometimes refer to checking the following card in the combinations provided.

You can use the four-card formation with or without specific questions. If you're feeling adventurous, you could create your own spread with two or three sets of the four-card formation and give each set a title, such as "love," "work," or "finances," etc., depending on what you wish to explore, you could also cover general readings without set questions. (Eagle-eyed readers will note this is how my Life Spread came into being!)

Examples of Connecting Cards and Combinations
As you progress, together with the information in chapters two and three, the following examples provide a sense of how we can start to fit all the pieces together.

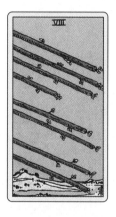

Keywords: News coming in quickly > Offer or proposal >
Joint venture > Progress and expansion

First impression: Positive. Multiple Wands suggest action, enterprise, and a swift pace. There are no multiple numbers or overlapped meanings and it flows easily.

The Eight of Wands in the present position shows good news coming in quickly; we know it's good because it's followed by positive cards. The message brings an offer or proposal to become involved in a joint venture, which could be a business partnership or group venture. This could do well for the client, as it shows the initial stages of success being achieved, allowing further plans to be made for the future. It should enable them to expand their activities and make good progress, so this is an offer worthy of consideration.

Let's look at a slightly different picture:

Keywords: Offer or proposal > Uncertainty, secrecy >
Hidden agenda, secrecy > Disappointment

First impressions: Negative. Reinforced meaning of secrecy and possible deception. Two Fives suggest instability.

In this instance, an offer or proposal received may leave the client feeling uncertain how to proceed, but there's also an overlap in the meaning of secrecy with the Moon and Five of Swords, suggesting they're not being given the full story and something is being hidden. If they proceed, it appears it would be to their detriment, and they may be taken advantage of in some way. Something is not aboveboard and would lead to regrets and disappointment. The two Fives also indicate instability, which adds to the uncertain and unstable elements of the Moon.

How to Use This Book and What's Inside

This book is based on the relationships between card meanings and intended as a guide to assist you as you work through your readings, so you can refer to it or dip in and out as needed. So far as possible, the information is presented so you can find most of what you need under the one card. Due to the nature of combinations, cross-referencing may be required at times, to avoid repeat or duplicate information as much as possible.

There are various levels and different types of combinations available in a reading, so there are numerous areas provided for your reference. Within each card section, you'll find the following:

Suit Element

Suits present, dominant, or even by their absence can help highlight a particular area of life. Dominance of a suit is usually one of the first things we learn to look for in our readings and can help point us in the right direction or keep things on track.

Flow

Flow can help to provide an overview of how events will unfold over the given timeframe for the reading (six months, for example), how fast or slow certain matters may occur when interacting with other cards, or blockages that may be evident due to the influence or appearance of certain cards.

Polarity (Type)

Most cards can be considered to have both good and shadow sides, which can be dependent upon the influence of surrounding cards. However, in the context of reading a combination, we can generally divide them into three camps of positive, negative, or neutral. Identifying polarity can be helpful as a first impression or when needing to break something down if the reading isn't making sense. All cards are influenced by those surrounding, but the cards listed as neutral can be more reliant upon (and affected by) the effect of other cards, determining which way they fall.

Multiple Numbers

Multiple numbers appearing in a spread can also offer additional insight into a theme. Although I have provided all of them, the most significant ones I tend to use are the Aces, Fives, Sevens, Nines, and Tens.

Keywords and Phrases

Keywords are the core meaning and concept for the card. Saying just a few keywords to yourself as you lay the cards down can help in the following ways:

- Improves familiarity to help with recall and instant recognition
- Acts as a memory jogger to trigger the wider interpretation
- Retains focus; keeps your conscious mind occupied to help prevent overwhelm or going blank, whilst allowing your subconscious to work unfettered
- Provides a first impression and quick overview of what you're dealing with before expanding further
- Creates a framework for the rest of your reading and intuition to lay over the top
- Highlights similar cards, repeat meanings, and shared connections within the spread
- Reveals the flow of the reading and how it will transfer to the client's life and experiences moving forwards
- Sometimes you'll find that the cards appear to read easily and smoothly, like a statement, just from the keywords alone.

Applied Meaning

This section covers interpretations for each card and different ways they may apply to your reading, both in different settings and how they can be affected by other cards, as applicable. Where appropriate, I have offered some personal tips and words of advice gained from my reading experiences. We're using the Rider-Waite-Smith, as the continued popularity of this iconic deck, first released in 1909, has inspired many of the modern decks that have since followed, which should make it easier for any adaptions you may wish to make with your chosen deck.

Reversed or Badly Aspected

Historically, reversals were a later addition and remain a matter of personal choice; some readers like to use them and others don't. I initially worked with reversals for around fifteen years but haven't done so since, as I found the results better without, so it's just my preference. There is light and shadow in all the cards with a full spectrum and range in between, and once you become adept at blending and linking cards together, you start to see the more subtle nuances of their relationships together.

"Badly aspected" refers to the kind of relationship in which an upright card is affected negatively by those following or surrounding it, as though it is hemmed in or imprisoned by other cards to thwart it. A badly aspected card is similar to having a bright lamp in the room and throwing a cloth over it: the light is still there but is dim and muted. The card is blocked in some way, similar to how some people read reversals—that is, they don't always show a complete reversal to the meaning.

If you prefer to work with reversals, you can either switch one of your cut piles before shuffling to ensure you have some or only read them if they naturally appear reversed (the latter was my personal preference when I did use them). I have included some brief meanings for reversals or badly aspected cards, but the latter is usually dictated by the meaning of the card following.

Associations

This grouping relates to categories of similar and opposing cards—how they relate to one another or not, followed by combinations. Associations apply in all layouts but should prove particularly useful for those of you who work with larger spreads—the more cards you use, the higher the probability they will occur. Associations are integral to the way I read with my signature spread, the Life Spread and Anchor, as featured in the other *Easy Tarot* books, making them especially helpful for those of you who also use it.

Similar and Supporting Cards

One of the easiest ways to work with combinations is to look for cards that have a similar and overlapping meaning to reinforce that interpretation in the reading. The cards don't always need to be side by side when used in a larger spread, and it can provide additional insights to indicate something the client should be aware of, such as an increase in finance, secrecy, or travel, for instance.

When considered collectively in the spread, the presence of repeating themes can provide another dimension or an underlying message for your client. Some of the cards have secondary meanings or multiple ways in which they can be applied, so the repetition of a similar theme can also help to clarify which direction to take with an interpretation, almost as though they're backing each other up.

Opposing and Contradictory Cards

Cards which appear to oppose or contradict one another often show circumstances working against one another and may represent opposing forces in a situation. These types of indications tend to reflect a choppy flow, or it seems as though the previous card is running straight into a brick wall of the card following it, thus showing opposition or challenges with upcoming events.

If you've ever experienced a set of cards that appear to be at odds with each other and at first don't seem to make sense, it can often point to contradictory circumstances arising. Life can be messy; sometimes the cards can be literal in their reflection of this fact as they jump from one subject to another, suggesting intervening yet unrelated events. Opposing cards can also show turnaround situations, both good and bad.

Featured Combinations

Card combinations enhance rather than change the card interpretation, which is why you don't need to learn or memorise lists of particular cards together. The combinations shared with you here provide a full range as we gradually progress through the book, from simple pairs to more complex and detailed arrangements involving three to five cards, to demonstrate how they meld together. I hope this helps to clarify things in your own mind as you begin to get a sense and feel for them.

These combinations are real examples that I use and have seen in readings but are not set in stone. As with all readings, there are many variables to consider, such as the spread used, the question asked, how it relates to the client's background, surrounding cards and, perhaps most importantly, the meanings you have assigned to each card. All readers work a little differently, but these combinations should give you a flavour and starting point as you work through them.

To avoid repeat information, not every combination involving each card is shown under its own section; aside from a few notable exceptions, few repeats are given. There are certain cards that need little explanation with their positive or negative connotations, so it would seem unnecessary to list every possible pair as a combination.

It can be tempting to provide some rather creative combinations, but I wanted to show a true reflection of the kind of situations that mainly turn up in real situations. I can only speak from personal experience, but I've found that regardless of country, culture, background, or financial status, the concerns most people wish to know about and address are remarkably similar, namely: buying or selling property, improvement of finances or related hiccups, starting a business or launch, starting or leaving a job, workplace issues, all manner of legal situations, and every shade of relationship matters for love, family or interpersonal. For this reason, these are the main areas you will find within the combinations.

Combinations for each card are shown with an arrow symbol > to indicate the cards that follow it. Unless otherwise stated, the ordering is important to the overall interpretation.

Making Friends with Your Deck

When you lay down your cards, they're responding to the personal language you share with your subconscious, similar, perhaps, to dreams. There may be universal archetypes, but there are also meanings unique to you, garnered from your own life experiences. And so it is or will be with your tarot deck: a shared secret language based on *your* intention—the meaning you specifically allocate to each card. For me, at least, this is the space where the magic happens!

One of the "rules" of reading tarot is that there are no rules as such. There may be accepted norms and set systems from particular schools of thought or popular theories, but there are no absolutes or limitations, except those you set for yourself. It really helps to become acquainted and comfortable with your chosen deck, so your cards feel like longtime friends, reflections of familiar faces in the dance of life.

I tend to view my tarot as a set of travelling players, a mobile theatre company that lives in my bag, just waiting to be released onto the stage to tell their story. They have individual characteristics, wise or witty thoughts; some can be quite chatty, solemn, or opinionated, and when I'm reading for myself we have full-blown conversations! So without further ado, let me help bring these cards to life for you.

II

The Minor Arcana
Applied Meanings and Combinations

ACE OF WANDS

Wands Suit: Action and anterprise. Action oriented. High energy.

Element: Fire. Active. Male energy.

Flow: Swift and fast pace

Polarity: Positive

Multiple Aces: Indicates conditions that bring lots of new beginnings and fresh starts across the board. All four in the reading can show a clean sweep and total change of lifestyle.

Keywords and Phrases: Exciting new beginning. New venture or work. A whole new way of life.

Applied Meaning

The Ace of Wands holds all the potential of the fire element in the suit, so whatever transpires is usually surrounded by plenty of movement, enthusiasm, and excitement. Wands represent action and enterprise, so they are often (but not always) related to work and career matters, an area in which we usually dedicate a good deal of our energy. As Aces represent something beginning, the simplest interpretation would be the start of a new work project or an exciting new enterprise.

The Ace of Wands is full of zeal, bursting with energy, and firing on all cylinders. The flame of your ambition burns brightly and can bring a rush of creative thoughts or new ideas but, whilst it's fizzing and popping with potential, it will also require action to follow through beyond the initial concept. Similar to striking a match, if you don't take action with it, it will quickly burn out.

In relationships, this card can ignite a surge of passion, whilst alongside a new romance may indicate an exhilarating and passionate affair of the heart with physical and fiery desires—when connected to a new relationship, look for something solid following to stabilise beyond the initial flush.

In home and family life, the Ace of Wands can indicate a whole new way of life that is eagerly embraced; with the right cards, it can suggest the actual beginning of a new life with conception and pregnancy (see the Empress).

Multiple Aces appearing anywhere across a larger spread indicates lots of new beginnings afoot that will affect various areas of life. If endings are present, look for the Aces to show if and how much further on a new beginning follows. In simple lines or free-flow spreads, look to the card following to see where the new start may lead and how it progresses. If an unfavourable card immediately follows, it can show a false start, or something new that wouldn't materialise as it should.

Reversed or Badly Aspected

A false start, blocks and failure of plans to ignite, scattered thinking due to too many ideas not acted upon, impetuous or reckless action in the heat of the moment, flash in the pan, enthusiasm and momentum fizzles out, lack of commitment. Feeling frustrated and impotent (sometimes actual impotence in the right context), creative (writer's) block, uninspired or lack of imagination, delays, running into a brick wall.

Card Associations

Similar and Supporting Cards: All the **Aces** represent new beginnings; **the Fool** is often also present. **Eight of Pentacles** (new work), **the Star** (inspiration), **the Chariot** (charging out the gate), **the Magician** (initiating action).

Opposing and Contradictory Cards: Death and **Ten of Swords** (endings), **Four of Cups** (apathy, uninspired), **the Moon** (uncertainty, wavering). The **Six of Cups** and **Judgement** both suggest something from the past or resurrected, rather than brand new.

Ace of Wands Featured Combinations

Ace of Wands > Two of Wands: The start of a new business partnership or work collaboration. Initial steps being taken towards getting a new project off the ground.

Ace of Wands > Three of Wands: A new venture (or job) brings quick accomplishment with first stages of success being achieved. New business starting to trade and plans for commercial expansion.

Ace of Wands > Eight of Cups: In due course this new endeavour will not last and you will walk away from it within quite a short timeframe, perhaps for good reason.

Ace of Wands > Ace of Swords: New ideas and projects find strength of purpose, good ideas and decisive action.

Ace of Wands > Two of Swords: Procrastinating or faltering, being indecisive as to how to move your new venture forwardss, new project stalls.

Ace of Wands > Page of Swords: May not get off to a quick start as some minor delays or slightly disappointing news indicated. Also ...

Ace of Wands > Page of Swords > Five of Swords: ... a troublemaker or gossipmonger trying to create problems for you in a new venture—watch your back.

Ace of Wands > Five of Pentacles > Five of Cups: A new venture could prove more expensive than initially anticipated with unexpected expenses, or a lack of funding may prevent matters getting off the ground at all, but this project fails to live up to your hopes as it leads to disappointment and regrets. (Two Fives also add to instability.)

Ace of Wands > Eight of Pentacles: New work (an overlap and reinforced meaning strengthens the interpretation), start of a new course of study to enhance skills, can be a whole new way of life for a formal education student.

Ace of Wands > Ten of Pentacles: Starting a business from home. Opening a property or family business. New work based at home. An exciting new beginning that brings stability to the family, possibly a new home but most especially when the Knight of Wands is also present.

Ace of Wands > the Lovers: A passionate new love relationship, could meet a partner through new work/project (if single). A new start that leads to love. A new beginning that will involve your partner, a possible business venture together (for those attached).

Ace of Wands > Justice: Can bring legal documents, agreements, or contracts; a new business contract, a new work contract. Balance action with objective thought.

TWO OF WANDS

Wands Suit: Action and enterprise. Action oriented. High energy.

Suit Element: Fire. Active. Male energy.

Flow: Swift pace

Polarity: Positive

Multiple Twos: Continuation, development, partnership, balance.

Keywords and Phrases: Moving forwards with plans. Joint ventures, working partnership, collaboration.

Applied Meaning

The Two of Wands takes up the baton to continue the journey from the Ace, the point where a commitment is made to follow through and take the first tentative steps. Initial plans are being formulated and action taken towards them. The two Wands in this card appear quite literal, representing something becoming established and made concrete, as one has been secured to the castle ramparts and the other is held firmly in the man's grasp. Just as the man contemplates his journey, the globe and confident stance suggest a level of preparation in readiness for the path ahead of his worldly ambitions. This is the point where the rubber meets the road!

The seed of the idea from the Ace is now being worked with and made manifest, taking root and starting to grow, although it is still in the early stages and the end result may seem far away. It can represent the first phase in developing plans and awareness of an as-yet-unknown future of the journey ahead. You may start to see the first fragile green shoots of growth, but your focus lies beyond to the unfolding horizon of your new ambition, fuelled by enthusiasm and belief in your plans.

This is the main indicator card I would look for to signify joint ventures, a business partnership, project collaborations, a cooperative, group endeavours and working with others collectively, pulling together and being united in a common goal.

Reversed or Badly Aspected

Plans stall or have difficulty getting off the ground. Difficulties connected to a business partner, lack of cohesion with work colleagues, or feeling held back by others. Wavering focus, unreliable or non-committal.

Associations

> **Similar and Supporting Cards: Two of Pentacles** (balancing energies), **Temperance** (cooperation). To some extent the **Three of Cups** (group activity), and **Two of Cups** (but romantic partnership rather than enterprise).

> **Opposing and Contradictory Cards: Five of Wands** (rivalry), **Four of Cups** (apathy), **Two of Swords** (stalemate, stalling), **Four of Pentacles** (holding back), **the Hanged Man** (immobility), **the Moon** (uncertainty), **the Hermit** (thought rather than action; solitary rather than collaborative).

Two of Wands Featured Combinations

Two of Wands > Five of Wands: Rivalry in a working partnership with opposing views, working against each other, a conflict of interests. Initial plans start to hit obstacles.

Two of Wands > Six of Wands: Early efforts achieve recognition and popular support. Business partnerships and working groups may receive an award.

Two of Wands > Seven of Wands: Doubling up on your commitment and belief to see something through, defending the integrity of your plans or feeling the need to hold firm on your position with a working partner.

Two of Wands > Two of Cups: A working partnership could become more personally involved. Taking active steps towards developing and deepening a relationship. For those attached, it can indicate partners in both work and love.

Two of Wands > Nine of Cups: Dream team. An early win and fulfilment of an initial goal.

Two of Wands > Four of Cups: May soon become disheartened and lose enthusiasm over preliminary plans. Feeling jaded with a work partner. Early efforts run out of steam and fall flat.

Two of Wands > Three of Swords: Quarrels in a joint venture, moving things forwards leads to upheaval and upsets.

Two of Wands > Four of Swords: A brief pause to pull resources together quite soon after the initial roll-out, an incubation period before continuing further.

Two of Wands > Ace of Pentacles: Partnership contract or financial agreement, important document in connection with your plans, the opportunity to secure a good foundation for the future. (Justice can also indicate a formal legal contract).

Two of Wands > Two of Pentacles: Multiple business partners, careful cash flow in a business partnership, balancing the books. Keeping plans flowing.

Two of Wands > Five of Pentacles: A business partnership or joint venture runs low on funds; this project may be more costly than first anticipated.

Two of Wands > Six of Pentacles: A charitable group or cooperative, favourable conditions and generous benefactors sympathetic to your cause. In business partnerships it may represent an angel investor or silent partner.

Two of Wands > Knight of Pentacles: Methodical application to the task at hand, plodding along taking care of practical measures, may take some time to get the ball rolling—not a quick fix.

Two of Wands > the Devil: If a working partnership then check all is aboveboard, most particularly if the Five of Swords is also present. Whether a working relationship or moving forwards with plans, you may have trouble extricating yourself later or discover you're tied into something you'd rather not be! Due diligence is required.

Two of Wands > Death: Forwards plans cancelled, a halt to proceedings, a working partnership ending.

Three of Wands

Wands Suit: Action and enterprise. Action oriented. High energy.

Element: Fire. Active. Male energy.

Flow: Swift pace

Polarity: Positive

Multiple Threes: Growth, expansion, progress.

Keywords and Phrases: Small success, progress and expansion.
  Trade and commerce.

Applied Meaning

Following the journey from the Ace, the developing plans actioned in the Two now find a foothold and gain some traction. The two Wands featured in the previous card now sit in the ground behind the merchant, indicating he has successfully passed that point as he firmly holds a third Wand beside him. His clothing reflects an improved status as his focus turns towards the ships setting sail across the horizon, perhaps carrying his merchandise or exploring new territories as he remains on firm ground.

The Three of Wands indicates progress and brings the first flush of accomplishment in your goals, as the details start to slot together and fall into place. Although success is on a smaller scale than found in the World, for instance, it is still an important stepping-stone along the way and in the right direction, an important milestone to a larger goal.

Whatever you have been working towards will find its feet; momentum is gathering. Seeing results emerge adds confidence to your thoughts and goals as you are now in a stronger position, providing a clear path to move onto the next phase of planning for the future. The confidence from initial progress leads to consideration of growth and expansion to your plans and this may be in any area of life.

In business and career matters the Three of Wands is the main indicator for trade and commerce situations, merchants, industry, and commercial business ventures.

Reversed or Badly Aspected

Difficulty with trade arrangements; setbacks and delays in plans; the inability to plan ahead due to challenges.

Associations

Similar and Supporting Cards: The Magician (confidence), the Chariot (triumph), the Star (hope and optimism for the future), Six of Wands (rewards and recognition). All cards representing success would provide overlap and backup to strengthen the meaning, including the World (though on a much larger scale).

Opposing and Contradictory Cards: Five of Cups (disappointment), Eight of Cups (abandoning plans), Two of Swords (stalemate), the Hanged Man (immobility); Ten of Swords or Death would bring a halt to progress.

Three of Wands Featured Combinations

Three of Wands > Two of Wands: Expansion of plans will involve others (expanding the workforce or working partners), successfully establishing a business partnership, small success brings continuing development.

Three of Wands > Seven of Wands: Maintaining the integrity of your vision for the future, defending your ideals as you move forwards.

Three of Wands > Ten of Wands: Expansion brings extra responsibilities, could be inundated with extra work, next phase could feel uphill.

Three of Wands > Seven of Cups: Choices to make but don't get carried away on the euphoric wave of first success, big visions but grand plans could be unrealistic (check the following card). Alternately, could open up lots of pathways to choose from.

Three of Wands > Eight of Swords: Brings limitations to progress, false sense of security could lead to getting locked into something.

Three of Wands > Ten of Swords: Limited success, no further gains to be found from this plan/project.

Three of Wands > Four of Pentacles: Stepping back to check stability whilst doubling down on effort following some initial success. Ensure due diligence rather than overcaution to expansion plans.

Three of Wands > Seven of Pentacles: Progress allows future investments. If vice versa…

Seven of Pentacles > Three of Wands: … investments show good progress and early promise.

Three of Wands > Ten of Pentacles: Successful plans concerning family home or material matters. Attainment brings material stability (work/business). Commercial property or premises.

Three of Wands > the Hierophant: Commercial organisation, institution, or corporation, usually large scale. Can also indicate dealing with bureaucrats as plans move forwards.

Three of Wands > the Hanged Man: Future plans will be delayed, consider alternatives. Commercial orders could slow down or supply chain issues create pause and delay.

Three of Wands > the World: Expansion into International trade and dealings. Building towards successful completion, reaching the pinnacle fairly rapidly from this point.

FOUR OF WANDS

Wands Suit: Action and enterprise. Action oriented. High energy.

Element: Fire. Active. Male energy.

Flow: Swift but more relaxed pace

Polarity: Positive

Multiple Fours: Structure and stability.

Keywords and Phrases: Stability. Rest and relaxation. A short break. Wedding plans.

Applied Meaning

The first stages of the journey are now complete. Matters start to find structure and stabilise as a consequence of previous efforts, shown by the four Wands firmly placed in the ground. Whatever you have been working towards should now bring a sense of satisfaction with endeavours so far, sufficient to allow yourself a brief but well-earned pause in proceedings with some downtime to enjoy the simple pleasures of life.

The Four of Wands can indicate high days and holidays, a short break or long weekend, a time for rest and relaxation before resuming once again. It can highlight the enjoyment of gentle socialising in the good company of family or friends, pleasant lazy days; picnics, barbeques, festivals, etc. The countryside and country pursuits can sometimes feature.

In whichever setting you find the Four of Wands, it brings a settled quality to life with a congenial atmosphere, adding a feel-good factor and sense of stability to your life and affairs. As a secondary meaning and with other cards indicating marriage, it can suggest wedding plans due to the garlands and bower that adorn the Wands, a structure often associated with wedding ceremonies.

Reversed or Badly Aspected

The Four of Wands is one of the few cards that remains unchanged or is affected to a lesser degree if reversed. Depending on the card following, it can still be diminished if badly aspected.

Associations

> **Similar and Supporting Cards: The Emperor** (stability), **Ten of Pentacles** (family stability), **Temperance** (harmony and balance), **the Sun** (happiness). Supports all other marriage combinations, such as: **Two of Cups**, **Three of Cups**, **Ten of Cups**, **the Lovers**, **the Hierophant**.
>
> **Opposing and Contradictory Cards: Five of Wands** (discord/instability), **Ten of Wands** (pressure), **Four of Cups** (dissatisfied), **the Moon** (unstable).

Four of Wands Featured Combinations

Two of Wands > Four of Wands: Initial goals find structure and stability.

Two of Cups > Four of Wands > the Hierophant: Growth in a relationship leads to wedding plans, whereas ...

Two of Cups > the Hierophant > Four of Wands: ... may indicate a wedding and honeymoon.

Four of Wands > Three of Swords: Squabbles and upsets create upheaval to previous stability.

Four of Wands > Four of Swords: A country retreat and peaceful refuge, the slow life.

Four of Wands > Ten of Swords: Holiday plans are cancelled or ...

Four of Wands > Ten of Swords > the Hanged Man: ... holiday plans are upended and need a rethink; alternatives needed.

Five of Pentacles > Six of Pentacles > Four of Wands: A generous gift helps to stabilise finances after a material hiccup.

Four of Wands > Ten of Pentacles: A holiday home, particularly if shown as ...

Four of Wands > Two of Pentacles > Ten of Pentacles: ... as the Two suggests more than one home, whereas ...

Ten of Pentacles > Four of Wands: may indicate a family holiday.

The Moon > Four of Wands: Uncertainty shifts gears and matters become more stable.

Five of Wands

Wands Suit: Action and enterprise. Action oriented. High energy.

Element: Fire. Active. Male energy.

Flow: Stalled

Polarity: Negative/Neutral

Multiple Fives: Challenges and instability.

Keywords and Phrases: Petty obstacles. Rivalry and competition. Friction and tension.

Applied Meaning

As the halfway mark between the Ace and Ten, Fives are a delicate balancing act that often bring challenges but usually of a temporary nature. In a simple line, the card following will show if and how this may be overcome, but if negative it could indicate an escalating situation.

The Five of Wands scatters the energy and reveals the first challenge on what has otherwise been a smooth progression of events so far. Office politics, rivalry, conflicts of interest, or competing forces, can all be found alongside this card in various combinations. It's not so much that people are openly fighting, but everyone appears to have a completely different viewpoint, so it's difficult to find agreement, which creates friction and tension. This would not be the time to present an idea that needs support from others or introduce a brainstorming session; the term "herding cats" seems appropriate!

Petty obstacles or struggles can crop up and it may feel as though it's just one snag after another, which could be frustrating and sap your energy but shouldn't be insurmountable. On the home front and in relationships it may feel as though people are being awkward or challenging, although there may be external factors affecting the circumstances rather than family or partners creating it.

On a separate note, energetic and competitive situations can be highlighted, such as sport.

Reversed or Badly Aspected

Challenges increase to a higher degree and lead to disputes; litigation can feature for some. Rivalry can become quite negative, with seeds of misinformation sown to intentionally cause problems and upset. Alternatively, some consider this card reversed to symbolise a breakthrough.

Associations

> **Similar and Supporting Cards: Three of Swords** (upheavals), **the Moon** (uncertainty, everything thrown for a loop), to some extent the **Seven of Wands** (defensive); other **Fives** present would highlight overall instability.
>
> **Opposing and Contradictory Cards: Two of Wands** (cooperation, working together), **Temperance** (harmony and balance, compromise), **Four of Wands, the Emperor** (stability), **Six of Wands** (support and recog-

nition), **the Chariot** (triumph over obstacles), **Ace of Swords** (challenges overcome).

Five of Wands Featured Combinations

Ace of Wands > Five of Wands: If you start a new job or business you'll be entering a competitive field or environment. New ventures hit some hurdles and obstacles.

Three of Wands > Five of Wands > Five of Swords: Commercial problems, competitors using dishonest tactics—everyone wants a piece of your pie; possibility of hostile company takeover. Two Fives add to the instability.

Two of Cups > Five of Wands > Two of Swords: Relationship differences where no one is relenting, lack of agreement resulting in no progress. Also…

Five of Wands > Two of Swords: … differences stop play; a standoff with no change.

Five of Wands > Three of Swords > Ten of Swords: Differing opinions lead to heated exchanges and arguments; situation escalating and could go too far and lead to a disappointing ending. Back off if necessary—there are no winners here.

Five of Wands > Two of Pentacles: Can show a bidding war between multiple buyers; high competition. Alternatively, successfully maintaining balance to overcome challenges, although care will be needed to prevent a recurring cycle.

Three of Pentacles > Five of Wands: Office politics, rivalry in your work.

Five of Wands > Eight of Pentacles: Successfully winning over the competition for a new job or new work.

Five of Wands > Ten of Pentacles > Three of Swords: Family disputes leading to upheavals and upsets.

Five of Wands > the Chariot: To the victor go the spoils! Triumph over obstacles and competing forces.

Five of Wands > Temperance: Mediation of warring factions to solve differences through compromise.

Five of Wands > the Star: Challenges or differences will be resolved.

SIX OF WANDS

Wands Suit: Action and enterprise. Action oriented. High energy.

Suit Element: Fire. Active. Male energy.

Flow: Swift pace

Polarity: Positive

Multiple Sixes: Harmony and improvement.

Keywords and Phrases: Rewards and recognition.
  Great news arriving.

Applied Meaning

The horseman wears a laurel crown with a second attached to the Wand he holds aloft, to signify victory. This card can bring rewards and recognition with others applauding your efforts. In whatever situation this card appears it would suggest acclaim, you are the victor "riding high" with supportive people singing your praises. Whilst it can apply to all situations, the most common combinations are often found with work-related matters involving advancement, promotions, or awards. The Three of Pentacles can often be alongside and included for this meaning.

In olden times, the rider brought important news from the outside world, causing people to congregate in expectation; Waite suggests the figure may be a king's courier accompanied by footmen, so as a secondary meaning it can indicate the bearer of great news. Cards surrounding should help you to decide which interpretation to follow. If there are other cards across the spread that also highlight messages, it can add another layer to your reading in addition to the primary interpretation. For instance, the Pages as messengers strengthen the association of the secondary meaning, but the Six of Wands would add weight to the news arriving (similarly for the Eight of Wands).

Reversed or Badly Aspected

Difficulty in attaining what you have sought which may not come to pass, plans thwarted and delayed, inability to mobilise yourself through fear or lack of motivation. Allies may not be trustworthy.

Associations

Similar and Supporting Cards: Three of Wands (small success), the Magician (mastery), the World (success, though to a larger degree), the Star (recognition), the Chariot (victory), Three of Pentacles (work recognition), Pages and Eight of Wands (also indicate messages arriving).

Opposing and Contradictory: Five of Cups (disappointment), Five of Wands (lack of support, rivalry), Five of Swords (people not acting in your best interest).

Six of Wands Featured Combinations

Ace of Wands > Six of Wands: New work promotion. A new venture that brings recognition or popular support.

Five of Wands > Six of Wands: Winning out over the competition; a successful candidate with popular approval.

Six of Wands > Three of Cups: This party may be thrown in your honour; celebrating an award.

Six of Wands > Ace of Pentacles: Winning or being awarded a new contract that has a financial connection. Can also be shown with Justice instead of the Ace (legal contracts).

Three of Pentacles > Six of Wands: Can represent an award or special recognition in relation to appreciation for your main work. An internal work promotion.

Six of Wands > Six of Pentacles: Promotion and pay increase. Can indicate an award that also contains a generous prize.

Eight of Pentacles > Six of Wands: Appreciation for your efforts in new work can bring rewards or lead to advancement fairly rapidly, a new work promotion. Also ...

Eight of Pentacles > Six of Wands > the Magician: ... graduation, recognition for moving from apprentice to mastery. (The Magician and Six of Wands can be ordered the other way round. The Hierophant can also feature for college, university, or a recognised institution, etc.).

Ten of Pentacles > Six of Wands: Important news from family (check following card to see where this leads).

Page of Pentacles > Six of Wands: Can bring important messages you're pleased to receive concerning finances (reinforces overlap of meaning). News of a scholarship or academic award.

Six of Wands > the Devil: May be receiving public recognition for all the wrong reasons! Negative press and bad PR. Can be an element of infamy indicated through nefarious activity.

Six of Wands > the Star: Popular support and public recognition.

Seven of Wands

Wands Suit: Action and enterprise. Action oriented. High energy.

Suit Element: Fire. Active. Male energy.

Flow: Swift pace

Polarity: Positive/Neutral

Multiple Sevens: A change of cycle.

Keywords and Phrases: Defending your position, integrity and principles. Negotiations.

Applied Meaning

The Seven of Wands is often mistaken as being an aggressive or fighting card, but it's more on a metaphorical level, fighting for what you believe in rather than on a physical level. There are lots of clichés that can help to remember this card, such as: defending your corner, having the courage of your convictions, standing your ground, or holding firm.

It suggests that in some way you may feel challenged over something you feel strongly about—perhaps a line has been crossed and now you feel your integrity is at stake—or possibly a cause close to your heart that you feel passionate about. The Seven of Wands represents being authentic to your principles or a matter that is important to you and a red line you are not prepared to cross.

There may be challenges, but you are in a good position to overcome them (on the proviso that the following card is positive), so long as you go about matters in the right way. In simple lines, any of the negative cards following may show that your efforts would be in vain regardless (see below for some examples).

It may be time to be assertive and face up to challenges, to stand up inside yourself and present your viewpoint in the best possible way, so you may need to do your homework. It can suggest tough negotiations in career or business; you may feel your back is up against the wall, but you should have an advantage in the situation.

Reversed or Badly Aspected

Weakens your position; the inability to hold forth; self-doubt may play a part. Inflexibility and a fixed mindset, dogmatic to your detriment. Unnecessary defensiveness.

Associations

Similar and Supporting Cards: The Chariot (strength of will), **Strength** (inner courage), **Ace of Swords** (clarity of purpose). To some degree the **Nine of Wands** (perseverance and determination), and **Five of Wands** (competing forces, opposing views).

Opposing and Contradictory Cards: Four of Pentacles (holding back), **Four of Cups** (apathy), **the Moon** (uncertainty), **Two of Swords** (indecision), **Four of Swords** (withdrawal).

Seven of Wands Featured Combinations

Five of Wands > Seven of Wands: A competitive situation where you don't feel inclined to back down and are prepared to take a stand. With the right approach, you can be successful. Check the next card (if one follows) to see how matters progress; ideally you want to see confirmation for a good result!

Nine of Wands > Seven of Wands > Ten of Wands: It may feel as though you're running into a brick wall; this situation will wear you down and may not be worth the pressure it brings.

Five of Swords > Seven of Wands > Ace of Swords: Successfully defending your position and integrity against those who have tried to discredit or cheat you. Alternatively...

Five of Swords > Seven of Wands > Seven of Swords: ... handle this situation very carefully, as you may have been set up by others with a hidden agenda.

Seven of Wands > Ten of Swords: Fighting something that ultimately you cannot win.

Seven of Wands > Ace of Pentacles: Holding your position and successfully negotiating a new contract (sometimes Justice may feature instead of the Ace). Similarly...

Three of Pentacles > Seven of Wands > Six of Pentacles: ... successfully negotiating a financial payment/bonus/increase in your work.

Seven of Wands > the Hanged Man: You may need to re-evaluate your position and the situation. Similarly...

Two of Swords > Seven of Wands > the Hanged Man: ... despite best efforts, nothing changes; may feel damned if you do and damned if you don't. The Seven of Wands is locked in and trapped by two cards either side that reinforce one another.

Seven of Wands > the Moon: Be careful—you could jump the gun, as not all the facts are available yet. Take time before asserting your position.

Seven of Wands > Temperance: Diplomacy needed but compromise will lead to successful mediation.

* Collectively, watch for multiple Sevens appearing anywhere in the spread as they can point to a cycle change, particularly if the Wheel of Fortune is also present.

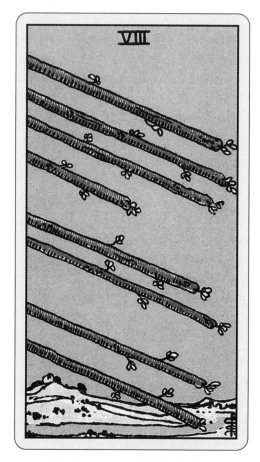

EIGHT OF WANDS

Wands Suit: Action and enterprise. Action oriented. High energy.

Element: Fire. Active. Male energy.

Flow: Swift pace

Polarity: Positive

Multiple Eights: Flow and movement.

Keywords and Phrases: News coming in quickly. Swift movement. Travel.

Applied Meaning

The Eight of Wands can indicate good news coming in quickly and will usually be followed by a good deal of excitement and enthusiasm. Communications are highlighted and can be in any form, although text messages and email are often the most common, being speedy methods of connection. If you're waiting for a letter or phone call, it should arrive very soon. In the right context, online dating could feature for some, especially when connected to the Magician and Lovers (example follows below).

In combinations for communication matters, in a simple line, check the card before to see where the news is coming from, and the one following to see where it leads. If a negative card follows, it suggests that news may not be so favourable. If the Eight of Wands follows a situation or is the last card, it may show swift movement and activity as a result of what came before. Activity levels increase and matters pick up pace in response. When accompanied by the Knight of Swords, everything is turbo-charged up a notch!

Travel may feature, particularly when accompanied by other travel cards, and may be connected to flying; in business matters, it can indicate air freight as well as internet and online business.

Reversed or Badly Aspected

Delays. Disputes, miscommunications, or disinformation. Poison arrows.

Associations

Similar and Supporting Cards: Knight of Swords (chaotic speed). All travel cards: **the Chariot, Six of Swords, Knight of Wands.** As messages: **Pages of Wands, Cups,** and **Pentacles,** and **Six of Wands.**

Opposing and Contradictory Cards: Page of Swords (delayed news), **Two of Swords** (deadlock), **the Hanged Man** (time suspended), **Knight of Pentacles** (takes time).

Eight of Wands Featured Combinations

Eight of Wands > Three of Wands: Can bring rapid progress and expansion. Whereas ...

Three of Wands > Eight of Wands: ... commercial correspondence, air freight; can also represent an online business.

Eight of Wands > Six of Wands: The swift arrival of important news (reinforces this aspect of the meaning found in both cards).

Five of Swords > Eight of Wands: Slanderous gossip or news you can't trust, as it holds an ulterior motive that will be to your disadvantage.

Three of Pentacles > Eight of Wands: Messages in relation to or from your work.

Eight of Wands > Five of Pentacles: An unexpected bill or expense arriving.

Ten of Pentacles > Eight of Wands: News from family, could also be concerning property matters (depending upon spread position or question context).

Knight of Pentacles > Eight of Wands: Long-awaited news finally arrives; things now move forwards with speed.

The Magician > Eight of Wands > the Lovers: Taking the initiative with online dating.

The Lovers > Eight of Wands: A love letter/communication.

The Hanged Man > Eight of Wands: Situation releases like a cork from a bottle! Swift activity after hiatus. News coming in after a long wait. Whereas…

Eight of Wands > the Hanged Man: … running into a "brick wall"-type situation where the brakes are slammed on. In communications, it can be a sign of ghosting, but look for other indications as well—it may suggest lengthy delays.

NINE OF WANDS

Wands Suit: Action and enterprise. Action oriented. High energy.

Element: Fire. Active. Male energy.

Flow: Slowing

Polarity: Neutral

Multiple Nines: Tying up loose ends, preparation for completion. Penultimate, almost there.

Keywords and Phrases: Perseverance, persistence, and determination.

Applied Meaning

The battle-weary figure appears to be making a determined stand to protect and defend the eight Wands planted firmly in the ground behind him, signifying his previous efforts to reach this point. The Nine of Wands is a defining moment in the journey where considerable effort has been made but a final push is needed to reach a finish line that may not yet seem to be in sight. In order to proceed, you will need to draw on all your resources and capabilities at a time when you may now be starting to question your ability to continue.

In whatever setting, it appears it can feel as though you've been constantly fire-fighting, determinedly soldiering on through the challenges. As the penultimate number of the suit, the Nine of Wands is the "almost there" card—it's time to dig deep. Perseverance will be needed but should pay off.

If the Nine of Wands appears as the outcome to your question, it may show that you're in for a long haul and the end result will require continued effort. In simple lines and free-flow methods, the easiest position is when this card acts as a bridge of sorts (middle card of three) where the card following shows whether persevering would be worthwhile. Ideally, we want to see a positive outcome where persistence pays off, so the more favourable the card following, the better.

Reversed or Badly Aspected

There may be endless obstacles that hinder progress and, despite considerable efforts, the situation doesn't work out.

Associations

Similar and Supporting Cards: Strength (endurance), **Seven of Wands** (standing firm, defensive), **the Chariot** (willpower), **Ace of Swords** (strength of purpose).

Opposing and Contradictory Cards: Eight of Cups (abandoning a path), **Four of Pentacles** (holding back), **Four of Cups** (apathy).

Nine of Wands Featured Combinations

Ace of Wands > Nine of Wands: Whatever you're setting in motion may take longer than you planned and will require persistence and determination. Check the following card, if applicable, to see if conditions improve; be ready to dig in.

Two of Wands > Nine of Wands: The road ahead seems longer than anticipated and requires all your reserves. A working partnership could become
wearisome and will take great perseverance.

Seven of Wands > Wheel of Fortune > Nine of Wands: It may feel as
though this situation is going round in a circle and taking you back to
square one; defending your position may feel like a continuous endeavour.

Nine of Wands > Two of Swords: The situation remains unchanged
regardless of efforts; time to reconsider your plans (similarly with **the
Hanged Man**).

Nine of Wands > Four of Swords: You will need to pull on all the resources
available to you to consolidate and strengthen your position. This will
take great effort and a restful period of recovery may be required after-
wardss. Take care to ensure that your health doesn't suffer in the process.

Nine of Wands > Ten of Swords > Eight of Cups: Persistent effort
finally results in a disappointing ending, but now you can let go and
invest your energy in a different direction.

Nine of Wands > Knight of Pentacles: This will take time, but you'll get
there in the end.

The Lovers > Nine of Wands: *"The course of true love never did run smooth."*
Persevering with a challenging situation within a love relationship.

Nine of Wands > the Star: The end is in sight with hopeful conditions;
keep going.

Nine of Wands > the Moon: Wading through fog; you're ploughing ahead
but things remain unclear—there are still unknown factors to this situation. Whereas …

Nine of Wands > the Moon > Three of Wands: … this could feel challenging, but after a period of uncertainty you'll start to see progress.

    * *Collectively, watch for other cards that suggest stressful conditions
appearing anywhere across the spread, to reinforce that aspect of the Nine of
Wands, particularly: Seven of Wands, Ten of Wands, Eight of Swords, Nine
of Swords, the Devil. Should any of these cards directly follow the Nine of
Wands, it may show a deteriorating situation.*

TEN OF WANDS

Wands Suit: Action and enterprise. Action oriented. High energy.

Element: Fire. Active. Male energy.

Flow: Slowing

Polarity: Negative

Multiple Tens: A period of completion.

Keywords and Phrases: Overwhelmed and overburdened, under
pressure. Burnout.

Applied Meaning

As the ultimate number of the suit, we see the result of too much fire; moving from the spark in the Ace to an unchecked raging inferno as the speed and movement of the element hurtles along and now overwhelms everything in its path. The Ten of Wands signifies too much of something that creates a heavy burden, such as too many responsibilities on your plate, feeling overwhelmed by a situation, financial pressure, or a burnout situation. The term "carrying the weight of the world on their shoulders," is a good analogy and can also be a warning not to make a rod for your own back.

In whatever area of life this card appears, it shows the client is feeling weighed down and under pressure, so look to the preceding card to see where the problem originates or what has created it. If there is a card following, we would hope to see the situation alleviating rather than progressing on the same trajectory.

Whilst the Ten of Wands is not considered a particularly positive card, it's important to keep things in perspective. For instance, I have seen numerous occasions where it has followed career matters and resulted in an influx of extra work, so the client was rushed off their feet and feeling overwhelmed but no worse than that. As with most cards, this Ten serves as a warning so you can prepare in advance or set up contingency plans.

Reversed or Badly Aspected

Can add extra weight to the upright meaning, although some see the reversed card as a relief from pressures. Badly aspected, we find a worsening situation.

Associations

> **Similar and Supporting Cards: the Devil** (bogged down, enslaved), **Eight of Swords** (restriction), **Five of Pentacles** (tough times), **Nine of Swords** (worries). Watch for any other stress cards (as outlined in the Nine of Wands entry).

> **Opposing and Contradictory Cards: Four of Swords** (rest), **Six of Swords** (recovery), **Four of Wands** (relaxation), **Temperance** (harmony and balance).

Ten of Wands Featured Combinations

Ace of Wands > Ten of Wands: A new venture may be more work than you initially anticipated: Are you biting off more than you can chew or is this an extra responsibility you can cope with?

Two of Wands > Ten of Wands: An imbalance in the workload with a working partner where you could be carrying most of the weight. Initial plans become burdensome.

Nine of Wands > Ten of Wands: Dogged determination that may not pay off, as it suggests a continuing uphill struggle.

Ten of Wands > Two of Pentacles: You may have a lot on your plate but should manage to keep all the plates spinning and balls in the air to keep matters flowing.

Five of Pentacles > Ten of Wands: Financial burdens, money worries increasing; overwhelmed by debts.

Three of Pentacles > Ten of Wands: Under pressure with work or in the workplace.

Eight of Pentacles > Ten of Wands: Feeling out of your depth in a new job or study course. For those self-employed, it can indicate lots of new work coming in that could prove overwhelming.

Ten of Pentacles > Ten of Wands: Family responsibilities weighing you down, can be connected to property matters in the right setting or context.

Ten of Wands > Strength: Stoic effort, valiantly struggling on despite overwhelming circumstances; carrying a burden with dignity and good grace; calm and quiet determination will carry you through, but don't be afraid to ask for or accept help to ease the load.

Ten of Wands > the Lovers > the Devil: Feeling pressured in a relationship, can suggest a manipulative partner or something unhealthy within the relationship that affects the client; look for further indications in the spread to reinforce this aspect. (Example of a trapped card—a positive card surrounded by negative influences.)

Ten of Wands > Wheel of Fortune > Eight of Swords: Feeling trapped in a continuous cycle or negative vortex.

PAGE OF WANDS

Wands Suit: Action and enterprise. Action oriented. High energy.

Element: Fire. Active. Male energy.

Flow: Swift pace

Polarity: Positive/Neutral

Multiple Pages: A flurry of messages, a group of children.

Keywords and Phrases: News concerning work. Outgoing child.

Applied Meaning

An easy way to think of the Pages is that in the royal courts of old, pages were usually young people who delivered messages and favours between courtiers. When it comes to meanings, Pages are the only court cards that have the possibility of being one of two things.

Primarily, the Pages bring news and messages relevant to their suit; as Wands indicate action and enterprise, this card usually brings news concerning work or project matters. Messages received are usually of a positive and active nature unless the card following is unfavourable, and by checking the card it leads into we can see what this news brings. If the card falls at the end of a line, this is the limit to what we can tell at the time of the reading; situations may still be formulating, but whatever comes next will be reliant upon that news being received.

As a secondary meaning, the Pages can represent children, usually minors (under the age of eighteen). The characteristics of a Page of Wands child is connected to the fire element; so they are generally bold, active, outgoing, confident, and sociable. Wands are "doers," so this Page likes to jump into things without much thought about what comes next.

In readings, I tend to find the Pages only appear as children when there is an issue surrounding them that also affects the client, so in the first instance I would usually work with the messages aspect first.

Reversed or Badly Aspected

Work-related news of a less favourable variety; messages going astray and communications awry. A rash or unruly child.

Associations

> **Similar and Supporting Cards: Pages of Wands**, **Cups**, and **Pentacles**; **Six of Wands**, **Eight of Wands**, as they can all represent messages.
>
> **Opposing and Contradictory Cards: Page of Swords** (delayed or minor disappointing news).

Page of Wands Featured Combinations

> **Page of Wands** > **Ace of Wands:** News concerning a new work project.

Page of Wands > Two of Wands: News relating to a working partnership, messages regarding an initial work goal. Early plans being made for an outgoing child.

Page of Wands > Six of Wands: Important news about a promotion or recognition at work. Outgoing child receiving an award or scholarship.

Page of Wands > Knight of Wands: News regarding relocation or travel arrangements for work matters.

Page of Wands > Ace of Cups: Message received through work leads to a new relationship (for singles); work-related news leads to a new beginning for love and happiness into the home (attached).

Six of Cups > Page of Wands: Communication from a previous workplace or an old work colleague.

Page of Wands > Two of Swords: The news you receive may leave you feeling undecided about a work matter; things are not moving forwards.

Page of Wands > Nine of Swords: Messages concerning a work matter leaves you feeling concerned.

Page of Wands > Six of Pentacles: News concerning a raise or bonus from work.

Page of Wands > Eight of Pentacles: News about a new job, or study placement for a child. Whereas…

Page of Wands > Knight of Cups > Eight of Pentacles: … correspondence with a new job offer or business proposition being made to you. A confident child receives an offer for a study placement.

Page of Wands > Justice: Legal papers connected to work, could be a contract or agreement arriving by mail.

Knight of Wands

Wands Suit: Action and enterprise. Action oriented. High energy.

Suit Element: Fire. Active. Male energy.

Flow: Swift pace

Polarity: Positive

Multiple Knights: Adds a lot of movement and activity.

Keywords and Phrases: Change of residence, work relocation. Travel.

Applied Meaning

An easy way to remember the Knights is that in olden times, they were the brave and bold defenders of the realm; they fought battles or were sent on quests, at the behest of the reigning monarch or sovereign authority to whom they served and swore allegiance. All the Knights appear on horseback, which further helps to remind us of the activity and movement they bring into play.

Knights represent an action or event of some description, and the Knight of Wands is the main card to represent a change of residence or moving home. Sometimes it can indicate home renovations, although it would usually be on a larger scale with lots of activity. If this card appears connected to work matters, it usually shows some form of relocation within the career environment rather than moving to another job.

For its secondary meaning, this card can also represent a journey that is often long-distance, so in certain circumstances it can be a combination of both, suggesting emigration. Some see this card as one of arrivals and departures.

Reversed or Badly Aspected

Delays and interruptions in all forms of activity and movement, particularly snarl-ups regarding house moves or a journey.

Associations

Similar and Supporting Cards: Ten of Pentacles (home/property). Any cards relating to travel: Eight of Wands, Six of Swords, the Chariot. Other Knights would reinforce an additional layer of movement and high activity level.

Opposing and Contradictory: Cards that show stagnation or slow movement, such as: Knight of Pentacles, the Hermit, the Hanged Man, Two of Swords.

Knight of Wands Featured Combinations

Ace of Wands > Knight of Wands: A new beginning that leads to moving home and an exciting new start. In career readings, new work that may involve relocation.

Ace of Wands > Knight of Wands > the World > Ten of Pentacles: Emigration and a whole new way of life for the family; international house move.

Two of Wands > Knight of Wands: Business trip with a partner; setting plans in motion for a house move or relocation of business.

Three of Wands > Knight of Wands: Expansion of business or career plans brings relocation. Progress with a house move.

Knight of Wands > Three of Cups: Celebrating a change of residence; a housewarming party. Travelling for a social gathering, usually a long journey.

Knight of Wands > Eight of Cups: Deciding not to proceed with a house move; walking away.

Nine of Swords > Ten of Wands > Knight of Wands: A stressful house move but you get there in the end!

Knight of Wands > Ten of Swords: Moving (or travel) plans are cancelled.

Knight of Wands > Six of Cups > Ten of Pentacles: Moving back to an old neighbourhood or one with past connections.

The World > Six of Swords > Knight of Wands > Eight of Wands: International travel that could be a world cruise or a trip with multiple destinations with various modes of transport indicated. (Reinforced aspect by three cards with a secondary meaning of travel.)

*   Collectively, in larger spreads (such as the Life Spread) when a house move is in the cards, there are usually more indicators in the spread regarding property transactions to back up the Knight of Wands, such as: Justice (legal papers), Ace of Pentacles (financial contract), King or Queen of Pentacles (money manager), King or Queen of Swords (the legal aspect), Knight of Cups (the offer), Ten of Pentacles (the property).*

QUEEN OF WANDS

Wands Suit: Action and enterprise. Action oriented. High energy.

Suit Element: Fire. Active. Male energy.

Flow: Swift pace

Polarity: Neutral

Multiple Queens: Strong female energy, women's group.

Keywords and Phrases: Outgoing lady, warm and cheerful, sociable and spontaneous.

Applied Meaning

The Queen of Wands type is warm and cheerful, sociable, and outgoing with a sunny disposition, preferring spontaneity to following instructions or a set routine. They like to keep busy and have a tendency to keep taking things on without really considering how they will fit it all in, which can cause them to be a bit scattered, disorganised, or forgetful. They act and talk quickly and are always busy and on the go.

If you have a Queen of Wands friend, she will often run late for your meetings but is such good fun it is hard to be annoyed with her. These types are good sports who are game for most things, being unafraid to laugh at themselves if it all goes wrong. The Queen of Wands often has a large group of friends or associates and enjoys socialising; they can strike up a conversation with anyone and like to be where the action is, so they may appear to have extrovert tendencies. The main characteristic giveaway is usually their outgoing but disorganised nature.

In predictive reading, the Kings and Queens come into their own as indications of actual people entering the picture. As such, it means they all have distinct and separate characteristics by which we can distinguish and identify them. They are also neutral—one element is neither better nor worse than another—but the circumstances surrounding the person will show how they affect the client and whether it will be in a positive or negative way. Kings and Queens are mature adults (eighteen and over).

If the Queen of Wands falls at the end of a simple line or as the outcome card—and it is not the court card chosen to represent yourself—it means that what comes next will be reliant upon the actions of someone of this description. If you identify with the Queen of Wands and have decided this card will represent you in the reading, it would mean the outcome is under your own influence and will be in your own hands.

In email readings, when you may not have the opportunity to discuss characteristics with the client during the course of the reading, it can be helpful to identify the parties involved by their astrology sun sign. The Queen of Wands could be taken to represent a woman having a fire sign: Aries, Leo, or Sagittarius.

Reversed or Badly Aspected

Can be flighty, irresponsible, self-absorbed, erratic, haphazard, chaotic, superficial, social butterfly, over the top, spiteful.

Associations

Supporting or opposing cards don't apply to Kings and Queens, as they're neutral and represent people of four distinct personality types.

Queen of Wands Featured Combinations

In combinations: Look to see what the Queen of Wands is bringing into the equation by the card following her, for instance:

Queen of Wands > Five of Swords: This outgoing lady is not someone to be trusted; she has a hidden agenda and is not acting in your best interests. Someone who brings deceit or dishonesty.

Queen of Wands > Page of Wands: News connected to work from a confident woman with a warm and outgoing personality.

Three of Cups > Queen of Wands > Queen of Cups > Queen of Pentacles: A social occasion with a group of women, such as a hen party or girls' night out.

Six of Cups > Queen of Wands: An old friend or colleague connected to your past who matches this personality type.

Ten of Pentacles > Queen of Wands: A woman of this description could be a family member or associated with a property matter in some way.

KING OF WANDS

Wands Suit: Action and enterprise. Action oriented. High energy.

Element: Fire. Active. Male energy.

Flow: Swift pace

Polarity: Neutral

Multiple Kings: Strong male energy, men's group or society, a number of men involved in the situation.

Keywords and Phrases: Outgoing man, dynamic, confident, bright and breezy.

Applied Meaning

The King of Wands type is warm and charismatic, comfortable in their own skin, confident and full of life. Wands have a pioneering spirit and are doers—they like to go out and make things happen rather than sit around and talk about it; they can have an appetite for adventure, and some may be thrill seekers or adrenaline junkies. They have a tendency to act first and think later, sometimes gaining a reputation for seeming impulsive. They are usually quite dynamic and exciting to be around—never a dull moment!

They see themselves as leaders and like to be forging ahead with big plans and ideas, but there's usually an army of people following behind taking care of the details. Detail is not their strong point, as it slows them down. They get bored easily and can flit from one thing to another, preferring a free rein with as few boundaries as possible. Wands are optimistic and quite resilient against failure or rejection, both of which barely register or are acknowledged since they didn't figure in their plan. They bounce back easily and continue ever onward with boundless energy.

The King of Wands has a good sense of humour and is usually happiest when surrounded by a crowd or being where the action is. Their warmth and charm tends to attract others and they can come across as quite bold or daring. The main characteristic giveaway can be their love of life but lack of planning.

In email readings when you may not have the opportunity to discuss characteristics with the client during the course of the reading, it can be helpful to identify the parties involved by their astrology sign. The King of Wands could be taken to represent a man having a fire sign: Aries, Leo, or Sagittarius.

Reversed or Badly Aspected

They can be self-centred, rash, careless, irresponsible, lacking self-discipline, impatient, hot-headed, arrogant, or vengeful.

Associations

Supporting or opposing cards don't apply to Kings and Queens, as they're neutral and represent people of four distinct personality types.

King of Wands Featured Combinations

The Kings and Queens are some of the easiest cards to read in a combination because they show *who* is involved and what they bring into the equation, which is valuable information for a predictive reading. In future positions, it can be someone not yet known but who will be recognised by their personality traits and circumstances that surround them.

King of Wands > Five of Wands > Three of Swords: King of Wands initiates a challenging situation that could be competitive and lead to quarrels and upheaval.

King of Wands > Knight of Cups > Eight of Pentacles: A dynamic and mature man brings an offer of new work to you.

Two of Swords > King of Wands > Knight of Swords: A situation that has been in deadlock is released by a confident and outgoing man; things move fast and decisively as a result.

Three of Pentacles > King of Wands: Mature man of this description connected to your main work. If no card follows, it suggests that what comes next will depend upon his actions.

The Devil > King of Wands > the Moon: There may be a lot this charming man (or lovable rogue) isn't telling you—he's surrounded by secrecy. Be careful and don't act in haste, as information will emerge in due course.

Ace of Cups

Cups Suit: Emotions. Love and happiness.

Element: Water. Passive. Female energy.

Flow: Gently flowing

Polarity: Positive

Multiple Aces: Indicates lots of new beginnings. If all four are present, a complete change of lifestyle.

Keywords and Phrases: New beginning for love and happiness. New romance.

Applied Meaning

All Aces represent a new beginning of some description, and Cups represent emotional happiness, making this Ace indicative of the beginning of love and happiness.

For those who are single, this is the main card I look for as the potential for the start of a new romance. For those happily attached, it suggests a new beginning that brings emotional happiness for all concerned (quite often through the home), bringing an outpouring of joy into the emotional life of both partners.

Although Cups tend to be the main suit we look for in connection with romance and relationship situations, they also relate to anything that may affect us on an emotional level. Their connection to emotions becomes more apparent as we move through the suit; Cups are thus not confined only to relationship matters.

Aces are like the powerhouses of their suit, brimming with possibility of all the ruling element represents. The Ace of Cups is like the beating heart of its suit, filled with the potential of the pure emotion it contains, waiting to find direction for nourishment and fulfilment.

There are many possible combinations connected to relationships, making this quite an easy card to link. However, they must be read in context with the surrounding cards, question (if relevant), and the client's existing relationship status. As part of a collection of other cards indicating marriage, this Ace can show the beginning of married life; similarly, a birth would usually be connected and surrounded by other cards indicating family, fertility, etc.

The Ace of Cups is often likened to the Holy Grail and due to the symbolic nature, some consider the Ace of Wands and Ace of Cups together as representing conception and pregnancy. My personal preference in relation to fertility matters is the Empress, so that is my focus and intention when reading, but combined with the Ace of Wands as pregnancy and with the Ace of Cups as a birth.

In the combinations that follow, different scenarios for either single or attached are indicated.

Reversed or Badly Aspected

Block to happiness, the empty Cup from which emotions drain away, unfulfilled (or unrequited) love, a false heart, sterility or infertility, lack of emotional nourishment.

Associations

Similar and Supporting Cards: All **Aces** indicate new beginnings, **the Fool** (completely new), **the Lovers** (love relationship).

Opposing and Contradictory Cards: Ten of Swords or **Death** (endings) **Five of Cups** (sadness).

Ace of Cups Featured Combinations

Ace of Wands > the Empress > Ace of Cups: The joy of a new addition to the family, expanding your brood (full-term pregnancy and birth).

Ace of Cups > Ten of Wands: A new relationship may prove heavy going or burdensome as things progress (single). A new beginning that signals joy may bring increased pressure or responsibilities (attached).

Knight of Wands > Ace of Cups > Ten of Pentacles: Move to a new home brings happiness and stability for all the family; this move is emotionally fulfilling for everyone concerned.

King of Wands > Knight of Cups > Ace of Cups: An outgoing man brings an offer of love to become involved with him (single). An offer or proposal from a dynamic man brings the potential for a lovely new beginning of emotional happiness for you and your family (attached).

Ace of Cups > Two of Cups: A new relationship deepening and developing onto the next stage (single). Emotionally this fresh new start has the support of both partners and will bring harmony into an existing relationship (attached).

Ace of Cups > Four of Cups: A new relationship leaves you feeling disenchanted fairly quickly (single). This lovely new start may not be all you hoped and leaves you feeling emotionally unfulfilled (attached).

Ace of Cups > Ten of Swords: Over before it's really begun, leaves a sense of disappointment.

Two of Pentacles > Ace of Cups > Seven of Cups: Choice of more than one partner in romance (single), multiple options surrounding the potential for a lovely new beginning although a joyful buoyancy can tempt your head into the clouds; a rational approach will be needed (attached).

Ace of Cups > Four of Pentacles: Fear of moving forwards with a new relationship (single). Feeling overly cautious concerning a new start; can indicate emotionally withholding (attached).

The Lovers > Ace of Cups: Love attraction that leads to romance (single). Couple decide to move forwards with a new beginning that brings joy and emotional happiness (attached).

The Lovers > Ace of Cups > Ten of Pentacles: Side by side and in any order, these three cards can represent marriage or serious commitment.

Ace of Cups > the Hanged Man: A new relationship stalls (single). Difficulty getting new plans off the starting line (attached).

Ace of Cups > the Devil: This may be one to give a miss; it can suggest an unhealthy relationship.

TWO OF CUPS

Cups Suit: Emotions. Love and happiness.

Element: Water. Passive. Female energy.

Flow: Gently flowing

Polarity: Positive

Multiple Twos: Continuation, development, partnership, balance.

Keywords and Phrases: Loving union. Harmonious partnership,
   deepening bond.

Applied Meaning

Similar to the Wands, we find a developing theme wherein what began in the Ace continues in the Two. As the Ace is the beginning of love and happiness, the continuance of the journey in the Two leads to a deepening emotional bond.

Some see this card as one for all types of close relationships, such as family or good friends who share a strong and harmonious connection. Due to defining down for divination purposes, this is one of the cards I reserve solely for love relationships; however, as with all the cards, I leave it to your personal discretion. The card will respond based on your intention.

In love relationships, the card signifies a strong rapport and deeply shared harmonious bond, a commitment to and continuation of the emotional journey. For a new relationship, it would suggest becoming more established and perhaps becoming exclusive; if already dating, there's a growing commitment to take the relationship to a more serious level, such as engagement, marriage, or moving in together, which surrounding cards should help to identify. For people already in a committed relationship, it represents a loving and supportive partnership with shared values and harmonious rapport.

If this card is found in a reading for someone who is single and the Ace of Cups is not present or it follows further in the reading, it can indicate the potential for a friendship to develop into a romantic relationship. This would be someone already known to the client and with whom they share a strong affinity; a preceding King or Queen may provide the identity of the person concerned.

Reversed or Badly Aspected

Challenges for a relationship, being out of step with your partner, a lack of harmony. A relationship that fails to develop; a lack of commitment. Infidelity or empty love; ships passing in the night.

Associations

Similar and Supporting Cards: The Lovers and all cards that support marriage, **Temperance** (harmony and emotional balance), to some extent the **Six of Cups** if suggesting someone already known (see next page).

Opposing and Contradictory Cards: Five of Wands (differences, at odds), **Three of Swords** (quarrels and upheaval), **Five of Cups** (letdown or betrayal), **the Devil** (unhealthy relationship).

Two of Cups Featured Combinations

Two of Cups > Eight of Wands > Six of Swords: Taking a trip together (the two cards following reinforce the travel interpretation). News from a partner that improves the relationship enough to move past prior challenges.

Knight of Wands > Two of Cups > Ten of Pentacles: Moving in together. For established couples, this home move will bring more stability to the relationship and family.

Two of Cups > Ace of Cups: Friendship blossoming into romance (single). You and your partner engage upon a new beginning that brings happiness to you both (attached).

Six of Cups > Two of Cups: Someone already known and connected to your past turning into something deeper.

Two of Cups > the Hierophant > Ten of Cups: A strong combination as an indication for marriage.

Knight of Cups > Ace of Pentacles > Two of Cups: Marriage proposal and engagement (proposal—ring—engagement).

Two of Cups > Three of Swords > Four of Swords: Quarrels and upsets with a partner could lead to withdrawal and time out. Whereas…

Two of Cups > Three of Swords > Temperance:…shows careful handling of a situation with your partner can resolve a disagreement; compromise may be called for—tread gently.

Eight of Swords > Two of Cups > Ten of Wands > Two of Swords: You may be feeling trapped and under pressure regarding a love partnership, perhaps undecided on how to proceed. Things won't change in the short term if you follow your current course of action.

Four of Pentacles > Two of Cups > Four of Cups: Counting the cost; the relationship may feel one-sided and leaves you feeling jaded. (Note how the Two of Cups is sandwiched and hampered by the cards on either side.)

Two of Cups > Ten of Pentacles > Five of Wands: The relationship is stable, but there could be some friction and tension with family members or concerning a property issue.

The Devil > Two of Cups > Two of Pentacles > Five of Swords: Could be more than one partner in this situation, and it is surrounded by secrets and lies.

THREE OF CUPS

Cups Suit: Emotions. Love and happiness.

Element: Water. Passive. Female energy.

Flow: Gently flowing

Polarity: Positive

Multiple Threes: Progress and expansion.

Keywords and Phrases: Celebrations, social occasions, friendships.

Applied Meaning

Whilst the Three of Cups is often seen as representing a wedding party, it can symbolise celebrations and festivities of all descriptions. In addition to weddings, birthdays, anniversaries, christenings, reunions, or social gatherings, it can also represent the happiness and sheer joy of something that brings cause for personal celebration, the moment you hear good news that leaves you feeling elated, such as getting a new job, an award, selling your home, or attaining a new one, for instance.

As a card of enjoyment and festivities, it highlights the sociable aspects of life and can suggest friendship groups and fun get-togethers, from formal functions to a good night out at a bar or restaurant, or meeting for a shindig and letting your hair down. The abundance of this three suggests that eating and drinking usually feature, sharing good times with family and friends at parties or social activities.

This lovely, cheerful card is very easy to work with in combinations: in simple lines, check the preceding card to discover what brings the cause (some listed below). In larger spreads, the area in which it appears should help to provide context.

Reversed or Badly Aspected

Excessive pleasure, overdoing it. Feeling excluded from group activities or by friends. Cancelled occasion or activities.

Associations

> **Similar and Supporting Cards: the Sun** (happiness), **Wheel of Fortune** (good fortune), **Nine of Cups** (wish fulfilment). Reinforces other marriage cards.
>
> **Opposing and Contradictory Cards: Five of Cups** (sadness, disappointment), **Five of Wands** (disharmony), **Four of Cups** (jaded), **Four of Swords** (withdrawal), **Nine of Swords** (anxiety), **the Hermit** (alone time). For some, the **Nine of Pentacles** indicates solitary pleasures.

Three of Cups Featured Combinations

Two of Wands > Three of Cups: Entertaining and social networking with business partners and contacts, wining and dining prospective clients. Making plans for a social event or special occasion/party.

Three of Wands > Three of Cups: Celebrating an early small win (commercial but can also apply to personal circumstances).

Knight of Wands > Ten of Pentacles > Three of Cups: Housewarming party for a new home. Can also represent travelling to a family celebration.

Two of Cups > the Hierophant > Three of Cups: Wedding ceremony and reception (wedding party).

Three of Cups > Four of Cups: A "party pooper," this occasion leaves you feeling flat; possibly an anticlimax.

Six of Cups > Three of Cups: Reunion party with old friends and colleagues.

Knight of Cups > Three of Cups: Invitation to a party or social gathering.

Nine of Swords > Three of Cups: Restored sense of joie de vivre; friends could rally round to help lift your spirits.

Three of Pentacles > Three of Cups: An office party. A work social event and informal get-together.

The Hierophant > Three of Cups: Religious festivities. (Can represent a wedding.)

Justice > Three of Cups: A legal matter rules in your favour and brings cause for personal celebration.

Three of Cups > the Devil: Wild night out, going over the top, the morning after the night before. May indicate toxic friends or a toxic social group, depending upon context.

Four of Cups

Cups Suit: Emotions. Love and happiness.

Element: Water. Passive. Female energy.

Flow: Blocked, stagnation

Polarity: Negative/Neutral

Multiple Fours: Structure and stability.

Keywords and Phrases: Boredom and discontent, indifference. Anticlimax.

Applied Meaning

The stability and structure found in the Four doesn't bode well for the water element, as it can turn stale and stagnant when contained. The Four of Cups is the card of discontent and represents feeling dissatisfied with a situation no matter how good the outward trappings appear to be; a sense of bored weariness leaves you feeling flat, jaded, or generally out of sorts. It can often indicate an anticlimax when following more positive cards.

Despite the magical offering of the fourth Cup appearing from a cloud, the youth in the image appears disgruntled and disinterested. The presence of this card can serve as a reminder that a sense of proportion may be required, and sometimes we need to recount and appreciate our blessings. It can also highlight the potential to miss a good opportunity due to apathy.

As an outcome card in a positional spread or the final card in a simple line, it tends to dampen the mood and suggests you may be less than thrilled with a situation's result. When surrounded by other cards, check to see what follows, as it may be pointing to good prospects that can help to improve matters, most especially when it shows there is something promising to be found as you may be at risk of just not seeing it.

Reversed or Badly Aspected

Renewed enthusiasm with fresh possibilities, a breakthrough moment with new solutions.

Associations

> **Similar and Supporting Cards: Eight of Cups** (disillusioned), **Four of Swords** (withdrawal), **Four of Pentacles** (withholding), **the Hanged Man** (life in limbo).
>
> **Opposing and Contradictory Cards: The Star** (optimism and hope), **the Sun** (happiness and contentment), **Three of Cups** (joyful), **Ace of Wands** (excitement and passion for something new).

Four of Cups Featured Combinations

> **Ace of Wands > Four of Cups:** Seemed a good idea to begin with; losing interest and feeling jaded as matters progress.

Seven of Wands > Four of Cups: May feel your point of view is being disregarded and lack enthusiasm to follow through any further.

Four of Cups > Three of Cups: Loving and supportive friends bring joy and good cheer. A situation you weren't enthusiastic about turns out better than anticipated.

Four of Cups > Eight of Cups > the Star: Underlying disillusion has been building and you may finally decide to walk away from a situation that has been draining you; this brings release and an improvement to circumstances.

Nine of Cups > Four of Cups: Be careful what you wish for; things may not live up to your expectations. Whereas…

Nine of Cups > Four of Cups > the Sun: …be tactful in your delivery, as it can reflect too much of a good thing or a lack of appreciation for the good that exists. You could have all you could wish for but still be dissatisfied.

Four of Cups > Eight of Swords > Nine of Swords: These cards warn of an escalating situation or downward spiral; dissatisfaction can become internalised and lead to anxiety if concerns are not addressed.

Four of Cups > Four of Pentacles: "All work and no play makes Jack a dull boy"; you may be working hard towards material goals, but check your fulfilment quota: something may not be ticking all your boxes. (Can also apply in the opposite order.)

Four of Cups > the Magician: Overcoming passivity and taking the initiative to move things forwardss.

Four of Cups > Strength > the Hanged Man: You may be making a valiant effort to plough on regardless, but matters need reassessment in order to advance. Be careful you don't become a martyr in your current situation or things will not change.

Four of Cups > the Fool > Wheel of Fortune: Be alert to a new and unexpected opportunity that can provide the potential for a complete turnaround to the situation; don't dismiss it out of hand.

Four of Cups > the Moon: Your present mood could be clouding your judgement and lead to uncertainty over how to proceed—allow some time for matters to clear.

FIVE OF CUPS

Cups Suit: Emotions. Love and happiness.

Element: Water. Passive. Female energy.

Polarity: Negative

Multiple Fives: Challenges and instability.

Keywords and Phrases: Disappointment. Sadness and loss. Regrets.

Applied Meaning

The Five brings us back to the pivotal point in the suit, an unstable factor where the following card can show if things will tip one way or another.

Traditionally, this is a card of sorrow and loss, not one we wish to find as the outcome or final card in a reading. In simple lines, the card that follows (when available) is the one most important to us, as it will show to what extent the loss will be felt and whether it is only temporary. Hopefully we will see cards that indicate a situation that "bounces back" or recovers; it's quite common to see recovery rather than an escalating or worsening scenario. If there is a preceding card, it can show where the problem originates and what may have caused the sense of despair.

The bowed figure appears to grieve over the three spilt cups, suggesting something emotionally ruined, but two upright Cups sit behind them, as yet unseen. Something is lost but something else still remains, although it may be further down the road before it becomes apparent. As is the nature of our human condition, we tend to focus on what has upset us, sometimes making us oblivious to all else.

The Five of Cups can show grief experienced after any form of loss that may affect us on an emotional level, not just matters of the heart: it could show feeling let down by others, personal regrets, or emotional disappointment.

Reversed or Badly Aspected

Healing and moving on from past hurts; recovery, but not usually the complete reversal of the matter.

Associations

Similar and Supporting Cards: Three of Swords (upsets), **Ten of Swords** (disappointing ending), **Eight of Cups** (disillusion), **Nine of Swords** (angst).

Opposing and Contradictory Cards: Three of Cups (joy), **Nine of Cups** (fulfilment), **Ten of Cups** (emotional contentment), **the Sun** (happiness).

Five of Cups Featured Combinations

Two of Wands > Five of Cups: Feeling let down or regrets over a business partnership or teamwork collaboration. Early plans suffer an upset and disappointment.

Five of Wands > Five of Cups: Guard against misunderstandings, as they could get out of hand and cause unnecessary upset. (Two Fives show the situation is unstable but usually temporary.)

Three of Cups > Five of Swords > Five of Cups: False friends and troublemakers; people not acting in your best interest leading to a sense of loss and betrayal. (For the identity of a specific person, the Three of Cups may be replaced by a King or Queen.)

Two of Cups > Three of Swords > Five of Cups: Can indicate a breakup, but could also be sharp words and a temporary rift (lower numbers and also the nature of the Five). With finality it would usually show as...

Three of Swords > Five of Cups > Ten of Swords: ... sadness and regrets over upsets that could cause a lasting chasm; if appearing in future positions it may be possible to take action to prevent matters escalating to this point. Or...

Three of Swords > Death > Five of Cups: ... would normally show finality to the split (quarrels—ending—loss), unless Judgement follows (see below).

Six of Cups > Five of Cups: Grieving for the past.

Five of Cups > Six of Swords: Moving on from a difficult situation; life will improve in due course.

Five of Cups > Temperance > Judgement: Healing, renewal, reconciliation.

Also watch for on-and-off situations where the cards appear up-and-down like an emotional roller coaster, e.g., Three of Swords > Temperance > Five of Cups > Judgement.

Five of Cups > the Moon: The upset causes confusion; in a sea of emotion where nothing seems clear, take time for yourself and don't act in haste. There are things not yet known that will become evident in the fullness of time.

Five of Cups > the Sun: A bounce-back or turnaround situation; the rift is only temporary. Alternatively, although initially it may seem all is lost, you will discover a hidden blessing as a result quite soon after.

Six of Cups

Cups Suit: Emotions. Love and happiness.

Element: Water. Passive. Female energy.

Flow: Gently flowing

Polarity: Positive

Multiple Sixes: Harmony and improvement.

Keywords and Phrases: People and places from the past. Memories. Nostalgia.

Applied Meaning

The Six of Cups indicates something from the past coming back into your life and, unless surrounding cards suggest otherwise, it usually holds fond memories. It could be old friends or acquaintances, but it can signify really anything with a past aspect. For instance, if you were looking to buy a house and this card appeared, it may suggest a place associated with your childhood or somewhere that you have a prior connection with. If you were selling, it may bring a previous buyer back into play; the key here is a previous link as opposed to something entirely new.

Old friends may get back in touch or you could be meeting up to reminisce with a trip down memory lane and recounting happy memories, so reunion occasions can feature. An old flame could reappear on your radar or back on your horizon, although for cards indicating reconciliation, I prefer Judgement as a strong indicator.

In work matters, the card can suggest a previous employer or place of work, a former field of work or skill set, old work colleagues, or business connections and associates you've had prior dealings with (some examples shown below).

Reversed or Badly Aspected

Living in the past, viewing the past more favourably than it deserves, rose-coloured glasses syndrome, refusal to let the past go, holding on to old emotions.

Associations

Similar and Supporting Cards: Temperance (renewal), **Judgement** (resurrection).

Opposing and Contradictory Cards: The Fool and **Aces** bring new beginnings rather than past aspects.

Six of Cups Featured Combinations

Six of Cups > Three of Wands: Reconnecting with old contacts or associates leads to progress and expansion (commercial); making future plans with an old friend (personal).

Eight of Wands > Six of Cups > Three of Cups: News regarding a reunion occasion with old friends; travel may also feature.

Six of Cups > Page of Wands: Good news relating to an old work project or from previous work connections.

Knight of Wands > Six of Cups: Moving back to an old neighbourhood or an area that has a special significance to your past. (Can also work in the opposite order.)

Six of Cups > Ace of Cups: New relationship with someone from your past and already known to you; can sometimes be an old love or a childhood sweetheart.

Six of Cups > Knight of Cups: An invitation from an old friend.

Six of Cups > Three of Pentacles: Work in a former field you were well-known for comes back into play. Whereas…

Six of Cups > Eight of Pentacles: … new work in familiar territory that may be an old workplace; or, a past contact leads to new work for you.

Ten of Pentacles > Six of Cups: Family reunion. May indicate childhood home.

Six of Cups > the Lovers: Someone from your past, or a former flame, stirs up fresh emotions with the potential to take things further.

Six of Cups > Temperance > Judgement: An old relationship renewed and revived. This is the strongest indication for questions about reconciliation.

The Moon > Six of Cups > the Devil: May have an unrealistic connection to the past that could become obsessive, trapped in a loop of nostalgic illusion that would not be healthy.

SEVEN OF CUPS

Cups Suit: Emotions. Love and happiness.

Element: Water. Passive. Female energy.

Flow: Drifting, meandering

Polarity: Neutral

Multiple Sevens: A cycle change.

Keywords and Phrases: Choices. Unrealistic desires, daydreams.

Applied Meaning

The Seven of Cups is our main card to show options and choices in the reading, although the extent to which they may be realised will be found in surrounding cards. In the positive, it represents the luxury of having options and the ability to make a choice, rather than matters being outside your control, so look for suitable cards that can ground the energy. In the negative, it can suggest an unrealistic viewpoint, fuelled by whimsical desires.

Imagination can run away with you or go into overdrive; in any setting, the best advice with this card is to carefully apply a healthy dose of logic and realism when considering the options available to you. Take practical measures and engage in a fact-finding mission, because the only truth you can rely upon are the genuine facts at the present time rather than what you think might happen further down the road, which in this case could be coloured by your desires or rationalisation that makes something fit a particular criterion.

The ordering of the cards can be important with these combinations (see below for examples), though sometimes it can simply point to a choice being available.

Reversed or Badly Aspected

Can show a clearer focus with an action plan, although some accounts increase the intensity of the upright card's negative aspects.

Associations

Similar and Supporting Cards: The Moon (illusions), **Two of Swords** (from the indecision aspect), **Two of Pentacles** (multiples).

Opposing and Contradictory Cards: The Emperor (stability, practical reasoning), **Justice** (balanced thought), **the Hermit** (discerning wisdom).

Seven of Cups Featured Combinations

Ace of Wands > Seven of Cups: A new beginning opens up other options as you move forwards, but these are early stages, so make a careful choice to prevent a scattergun approach (check other cards to clarify). These two can be a heady mix and need some grounding energy for all the possibilities and imagination they ignite to keep plans realistic. Whereas, in the opposite order …

Seven of Cups > Ace of Wands: … the advice is to take time to consider options: numerous opportunities are available to you. Your choice results in an exciting new start (could be work-related dependent upon question, position, or surrounding cards).

Seven of Cups > Ten of Wands: Feeling under pressure and overwhelmed by a choice that needs to be made.

Seven of Cups > Ace of Cups: Making a choice to enter a new relationship and can suggest more than one option (singles). Having weighed the alternatives, you set upon a new path that brings happiness for all (attached).

Seven of Cups > Eight of Cups: Despite the numerous options on offer, something isn't ticking all your boxes and you walk away.

Two of Swords > Seven of Cups > the Hanged Man: Dithering; indecision creates a logjam. Caught between a rock and a hard place, reassessment needed. Similarly …

Seven of Cups > Two of Swords > Eight of Swords: … analysis paralysis over making a choice; indecision creates deeper restrictions.

Two of Pentacles > Knight of Cups > Seven of Cups: More than one offer or invitation being extended to you; a choice will be required— take the most realistic option.

The Lovers > Seven of Cups: A choice needs to be made regarding a relationship. For those happily attached, it may suggest you will be making choices together as a couple.

Seven of Cups > the Hermit: Taking a cautious approach and doing research to carefully consider options and giving the matter a good deal of thought.

The Moon > Seven of Cups: Clouded thinking and uncertainty with how to proceed; appearances can be deceptive and all is not as it seems, so wait before making a choice—you don't have the true picture yet. In the opposite order …

Seven of Cups > the Moon: … watch for unrealistic pipe dreams; there is a risk of imagination and wishful thinking colouring your judgement.

EIGHT OF CUPS

Cups Suit: Emotions. Love and happiness.

Element: Water. Passive. Female energy.

Flow: Change of course, reverse flow

Polarity: Negative

Multiple Eights: Flow and movement.

Keywords and Phrases: Abandoning a path, walking away. Lack of fulfilment and disillusionment.

Applied Meaning

The Eight of Cups represents abandoning a path; it can be something you have poured yourself into, something to which you devoted a good deal of time, energy, or resources but now feels draining and lacks fulfilment. There can be an air of disillusionment or a sense of emptiness, and it may have taken a while to reach this point. But finally, you realise it would be better to focus your energy in a different direction to pursue a new path.

Something has run its course, but the decision to turn away is usually one of choice, rather than something enforced. It can suggest a point of realisation or a personal moment of truth when the penny drops: despite your best efforts, there is nothing further to be gained. This card is the moment someone wearily declares, "I'm done!" and can be relevant in situations where someone has continually invested themselves emotionally yet nothing changes, resulting in feeling spent through fruitless effort. All the Cups have been tasted yet found wanting— they lack emotional nourishment and cannot serve as sustenance, so the matter gradually declines.

This card can sometimes be quite straightforwards in a reading to show something being walked away from in any area of life. Whatever the preceding card represents shows what you are moving on from, whilst the card following reveals the path ahead and impact of this decision.

Reversed or Badly Aspected

Continuation brings satisfaction and enjoyment to the matter.

Associations

   Similar and Supporting Cards: Four of Cups (dissatisfaction), **Five of Cups** (sadness), **Six of Swords** (moving on), **Ten of Swords** (disappointing ending), **Death** (closing the door).

   Opposing and Contradictory Cards: Nine of Wands (perseverance), **Nine of Cups** (fulfilment), **Strength** (endurance), **the Star** (hope).

Eight of Cups Featured Combinations

   Three of Wands > Eight of Cups: Regardless of early success, it can signify a change of heart where something isn't stacking up and is causing you to walk away and seek a different direction.

Eight of Cups > Ten of Wands: "Out of the frying pan ... " possibly not a wise move at this time; walking away could bring additional pressure. In the opposite order ...

Ten of Wands > Eight of Cups: ... walking away from a situation that has become burdensome.

Eight of Cups > Five of Cups: Ensure you don't act in haste, as you could have regrets later. Here, the Five adds sadness to the sense of disillusionment.

Nine of Cups > Eight of Cups: This can be a tricky one; you may need to refer to surrounding cards for more clarity. Usually, it can show getting what you want but discovering it doesn't fulfil you after all. Occasionally—and depending upon other cards—this combination can be present when something good comes in that in effect releases you to abandon something else that drained you (more commonly the former rather than the latter).

Three of Swords > Eight of Cups: The quarrel may have only been minor, but it could also be the final straw that causes you to give up on the matter and abandon it altogether.

Eight of Swords > Eight of Cups: Calling time on a restrictive situation and your fears related to it.

Ten of Swords > Eight of Cups: Walking away from a disappointing ending with the realisation there's nothing further to be salvaged. (Look for a positive card following further ahead to indicate improvement.)

Knight of Pentacles > Eight of Cups: This situation may have been brewing for quite some time and finally comes to a head; walking away from a long-standing situation.

Eight of Cups > the Fool: Leaving an old path opens up the opportunity for a completely new one that may arrive unexpectedly. This would also be similar if followed by an Ace, to represent new pastures.

Strength > Eight of Cups: This may have felt like an endurance test and you've persevered with good grace but may finally decide to call it quits.

Eight of Cups > the Hanged Man: State of limbo; may not provide the release you anticipated as this path is not progressing.

NINE OF CUPS

Cups Suit: Emotions. Love and happiness.

Element: Water. Passive. Female energy.

Flow: Gently flowing

Polarity: Positive

Multiple Nines: Penultimate. Tying up loose ends, preparation for completion. Penultimate, almost there.

Keywords and Phrases: Wish fulfilled. Abundance and good cheer.

Applied Meaning

The Nine of Cups is one of the most positive cards in the deck; it's sometimes known as the "wish card," indicating that a wish will be fulfilled. This card is like a minor version of the Sun and one we would all like to see as the final outcome to our question, as it means we'll receive whatever we're hoping for.

Nine is the penultimate number of the suit, preparation for completion found in the ten; with Cups we find an abundance of joyful emotion. This card suggests that life is good and you feel sated, filled with the blessings you feel are being bestowed upon you. Whatever area of life it relates to brings satisfaction and emotional fulfilment, which makes it one of the easiest cards to read in combinations.

If the card appears in the present position, the client should already be experiencing the benefits. If they haven't yet, it will be imminent, although much will rely upon surrounding cards that could show otherwise. In a simple line, a card preceding will usually point you in the right direction of what the wish may be connected to. Sometimes the Nine of Cups can come beforehand (see below), so the card following would show whether the wish will come to pass and achieve full potential. The Nine of Cups is also one of the cards that often appear in "turnaround" situations.

Reversed or Badly Aspected

Reveals the imperfections or flaws of a situation that does not come to pass. Hopes remain unfulfilled. Pursuit of vanity projects.

Associations

Similar and Supporting Cards: The Sun (happiness), **Three of Cups** (good cheer and celebrations), **the World** (success fulfilled), to some extent the **Wheel of Fortune**, although this can be more ambiguous or fleeting at times. Most cards denoting happiness or comfort.

Opposing and Contradictory Cards: Four of Cups (dissatisfied), **Five of Cups** (sadness), **Five of Pentacles** (lack), **Ten of Swords** (ruined plans).

Nine of Cups Featured Combinations

Some easy combinations to denote a wish come true for the following (some can also appear in the opposite order):

Nine of Cups > Ten of Pentacles: Dream home.

Nine of Cups > the Lovers: Dream relationship or a "dream team."

Eight of Pentacles > Nine of Cups: Landing your dream job.

Five of Wands > Nine of Cups > Five of Swords: (Trapped card) You may win out against competing forces, but it will lead to a backlash and sour grapes. Watch your back for retaliation and dirty tactics. The two Fives highlight the instability of the situation.

Ten of Cups > Ten of Pentacles > Nine of Cups: The many blessings of family life and your cup runneth over!

Knight of Pentacles > Nine of Cups: A long-held wish finally comes true that could take some time but will be worth the wait. You have taken all the practical steps towards manifesting your desire.

Four of Pentacles > Nine of Cups: You have a definite plan for a material goal and are working hard towards it, which will pay off just as you hope.

Six of Pentacles > Nine of Cups: Receiving a much-hoped-for gift or one that may exceed your expectations.

Nine of Cups > Ten of Swords: Hopes dashed; perhaps it was not meant to be. If you receive what you want, it will be short-lived.

The Emperor > the Hierophant > Justice > Nine of Cups: Dealings with higher authorities that involve bureaucracy and the legal system, which will rule in your favour.

Wheel of Fortune > Nine of Cups: Fortune turns in your favour; a lucky break delivers your wish.

The Tower > Nine of Cups: What at first may seem a calamity becomes a blessing in disguise; this will turn out far better than you could expect but something needs to be removed before your wish can enter.

TEN OF CUPS

Cups Suit: Emotions. Love and happiness.

Element: Water. Passive. Female energy.

Flow: Gently flowing

Polarity: Positive

Multiple Tens: Completion of a cycle.

Keywords and Phrases: Marriage. Committed and contented love. Happy family life.

Applied Meaning

Our journey through the emotional suit of Cups brings us to the completion found in the final numbered card of Ten, therefore the ultimate for love and happiness. This card represents contentment in the heart department and all that can be desired in the realms of the heart.

The Ten of Cups is one of the marriage cards and is strengthened by cards of similar meaning. It can represent contented love with commitment being made, but also the comfortable satisfaction of a happy family life when surrounded by those we love. When someone is getting married, most of the supporting cards will also be present, so it is unlikely you would miss it! For those already settled, it indicates a happy marriage and emotional contentment in family life.

If you are reading for someone who is single and find the Ten of Cups but with no hint or build up to it, such as the Ace or Two of Cups preceding, it can show a whirlwind romance and one that becomes serious quite quickly. (There were examples of this in two of the real-life case studies in *Easy Tarot Reading*.)

Reversed or Badly Aspected

Can show stressful conditions within the marriage and family, an empty or loveless marriage as the emotion is drained out of the cups.

Associations

> **Similar and Supporting Cards: Ten of Pentacles** (home and family), **Temperance** (emotional balance), **the Sun** (great happiness). All marriage cards, or those that support it, would help to strengthen that particular association: **Two of Cups** (loving union), **the Lovers** (love partnership), **the Hierophant** (marriage, but can also suggest traditional family unit), **Ace of Pentacles** (wedding ring), **Justice** (official documents).
>
> **Opposing and Contradictory Cards: Three of Swords** (family upheavals), **Four of Cups** (dissatisfaction), **Five of Cups** (sadness), **the Devil** (unhealthy relationship).

Ten of Cups Featured Combinations

> **Ten of Cups > Ten of Wands:** Strain on the marriage or family; in some instances, both.

Ace of Cups > Knight of Swords > Ten of Cups: New relationship takes off quickly and develops at a rate of knots; whirlwind romance with swift commitment.

Three of Swords > Ten of Cups > the Hierophant > Temperance: Can indicate marriage guidance, counselling, and mediation services to restore harmony.

Ten of Cups > Ten of Pentacles: Emotional happiness and material stability; complete contentment in family life.

Ten of Cups > Judgement: As the second-time-round card, Judgement can represent remarriage, but can also indicate reconciliation (marriage resurrected.) Can also appear in the opposite order.

Look for other supporting cards in the spread. Indications of marriage can also include:

Four of Wands > Ten of Cups: Wedding planning and arrangements being made.

Ten of Cups > Four of Wands: Marriage and honeymoon.

Ten of Cups > Three of Cups: Wedding breakfast or reception, marriage celebration.

Knight of Cups > Ten of Cups: Proposal of marriage or permanent commitment.

Ten of Cups > Six of Pentacles: Wedding/marriage gifts.

The Lovers > Ace of Pentacles > Ten of Cups: An indication of marriage. *(More combinations for marriage can also be found on the pages for the associated "Similar and supporting cards," as listed previously).*

PAGE OF CUPS

Cups Suit: Emotions. Love and happiness.

Flow: Gently flowing

Polarity: Positive/Neutral

Multiple Pages: Numerous communications, group of children.

Keywords and Phrases: News of an emotional nature. A gentle-natured child.

Applied Meaning

The Page of Cups indicates messages with an emotional flavour that is usually news you're pleased to receive, unless it is followed by a less favourable card. Messages are not confined to only matters concerning love, so whilst it would be present for news of a romantic nature, it can also represent all forms of emotive news. As the card in a final outcome position of a positional spread, I would read it as happy news of an emotional nature, but at the end of free-flow or simple lines it may be a neutral card, since the cards before and after help to provide the detail.

When representing a child, Page of Cup types are gentle and sweet-natured, considerate, and thoughtful; they wish to please but can be oversensitive and get hurt easily. They can be a bit timid or unsure of themselves and require encouragement and reassurance.

Reversed or Badly Aspected

Emotional news of the less favourable variety; a self-absorbed child.

Associations

Similar and Supporting Cards: Pages of Wands, **Cups**, and **Pentacles**; **Six of Wands**, **Eight of Wands**, as they can all represent messages.

Opposing and Contradictory Cards: Page of Swords (delayed or minor disappointing news).

Page of Cups Featured Combinations

Ace of Wands > Page of Cups: Happy news in relation to an exciting new project or beginning. An exciting new start for a gentle, sensitive child.

Page of Cups > Five of Wands: Watch for miscommunications, as the message you receive could lead to misunderstandings, particularly connected to emotional matters.

Page of Cups > Five of Cups: An upsetting message that holds emotional disappointment.

Six of Cups > Page of Cups: A pleasant message from an old friend or possibly a former flame.

Three of Swords > Page of Cups > Temperance: An olive branch being proffered. You'll hear from someone you may have been estranged from, or possibly hurtful words were exchanged; with careful and diplomatic handling harmony can be restored, although some compromise may be necessary.

Three of Pentacles > the Hanged Man > Page of Cups: A work project, or situation connected to your work, may be delayed but you'll receive good news you'll be pleased to hear in the end.

Page of Cups > Six of Pentacles: Warm words and a kind gift you're pleased to receive.

Ten of Pentacles > Page of Cups: Family news, or a happy message concerning property.

Knight of Pentacles > Page of Cups: This may be something you've been waiting to hear about for some time; finally the news is forthcoming and leaves you well-pleased.

Page of Cups > The Empress > Three of Cups: Celebrating happy news concerning a pregnancy or birth.

The Lovers > Page of Cups: A love letter; news you're pleased to receive from a partner or love interest.

Page of Cups > the Moon: News or a message of an emotional nature may leave you feeling uncertain as to how to proceed. The content of this message may be clouded and not contain the whole story; the suggestion is that an element of secrecy and hidden information is involved.

KNIGHT OF CUPS

Cups Suit: Emotions. Love and happiness.

Element: Water. Passive. Female energy.

Flow: Flowing

Polarity: Positive

Multiple Knights: Plenty of movement and action.

Keywords and Phrases: Offers, proposals, and invitations.

Applied Meaning

As all the Knights represent a significant event or action and Cups represent the emotions, we therefore know that whatever the Knight of Cups brings must have an emotional effect in some way. Offers, proposals, or invitations of all descriptions are indicated. Whilst this card may bring an offer of love, a romantic invitation, or even a marriage proposal, it can also bring any form of offer that will affect you emotionally, usually pleasantly so.

With the Knight of Cups, the following card usually indicates what is being offered. In addition, the surrounding cards can show the effect of what they bring into play. In a larger spread, the area title may help narrow down where it is focused, whereas in a free-flow simple line, the card prior would point to the origin. In positional spreads, it would be one of the cards to look for if someone is specifically asking about selling their house or finding new work, as the Knight brings the offer.

Reversed or Badly Aspected

Less-than-ideal circumstances; an offer fails to materialise or progress; an unrealistic proposal from an unreliable source.

Associations

Similar and Supporting Cards: Will connect mainly to other cards of movement or to support emotional influences. The main factor can be with multiple Knights.

Opposing and Contradictory Cards: Stagnating or slow cards since most of the Knights bring plenty of action.

Knight of Cups Featured Combinations

Knight of Cups > Two of Wands: Could be a business proposal to form a working partnership or collaboration.

Knight of Cups > Ace of Cups: An offer of love (the Ace of Cups can sometimes be replaced with the Lovers).

Knight of Cups > Four of Cups: Anticlimax; an offer received fails to hit the mark or your level of expectation.

Knight of Cups > Eight of Cups: Leaving the offer on the table, walking away from an offer or invitation.

Knight of Cups > Justice: A contract being offered; this can also be the Ace of Pentacles.

Variations for marriage proposals can also appear as:

Knight of Cups > Ace of Pentacles > Two of Cups: Marriage proposal and engagement (proposal—ring—deepening bond).

Knight of Cups > Ace of Pentacles > Ten of Cups: Follows the progression to realisation (marriage).

Knight of Cups > Ten of Cups: Can be a marriage proposal or one of permanent commitment (not always marriage for some).

Knight of Cups > The Hierophant: An offer of marriage. Whereas, in opposite order…

The Hierophant > Knight of Cups: Can show a proposal or offer received from an institution, such as:

The Hierophant > Four of Pentacles > Knight of Cups: A loan offer from your bank (or similar financial organisation).

The Hierophant > Eight of Pentacles > Knight of Cups: Study placement offer from an educational institution, whereas…

The Hierophant > Knight of Cups > Eight of Pentacles: Work offer from a large organisation.

QUEEN OF CUPS

Cups Suit: Emotions. Love and happiness.

Element: Water. Passive. Female energy.

Flow: Gently flowing

Polarity: Neutral

Multiple Queens: A number of women involved in the client's life and whose action can impact or influence events.

Keywords and Phrases: Gentle-natured woman.

Applied Meaning

Queen of Cups personality types come across as mild-mannered, gentle-natured, and are often sweet or softly spoken. Cups are some of the nicest people you could ever wish to meet but, synonymous to the suit, they are creatures of their emotions. They feel things deeply, can be sensitive souls (sometimes overly so), and can easily feel slighted or take offence where none was intended. If you do upset them, it is unlikely they'd make you aware of it directly, since they seek to avoid any form of unpleasantness, but it can manifest as passive-aggressive behaviour or griping from the sidelines.

Queen of Cups people can be idealists, making the world seem a harsh place with all its trials and tribulations. The main giveaway characteristic is that they are lovely people but are not very strong and tend to avoid anything unpleasant like the plague. Your Queen of Cups friend will happily sympathise and listen to your problems but would never wish to be drawn into your fight or defend your corner for you.

For email readings, the Queen of Cups could be taken to represent a woman with an astrological water sign: Cancer, Scorpio, or Pisces.

In career matters, they do best in the fields of caring, counselling, creativity, public sector, charities, humanitarian, nonprofits, or non-competitive environments.

Reversed or Badly Aspected

May suffer from: victim mentality, codependency issues, insecurity, melancholy, childish, unrealistic, or delusional tendencies. Can be manipulative, saccharine, submissive, or weak.

Associations

Supporting or opposing cards do not apply to Kings and Queens as they're neutral and represent people of four distinct personality types.

Queen of Cups Featured Combinations

In combinations, a King or Queen may represent the client or someone who will be important to their situation; check to see what they're bringing into play with the card following them. The preceding card (if there is one) will show what brought them into the picture or what they are connected to. The extent of the effect they will have and whether it is positive or negative can be seen in the surrounding cards.

Queen of Cups > Two of Wands > Ten of Wands: If you're considering forming a working partnership or joint project with this easygoing lady, you may feel you're carrying most of the weight as matters progress.

Queen of Cups > Nine of Cups: A lady of this description will in some way be instrumental in bringing about the fulfilment of your wish!

Nine of Swords > Queen of Cups > Ace of Swords: A gentle-natured woman can be helpful with a situation that's worrying you and leads to a decisive resolution where you overcome challenges. Whereas…

Queen of Cups > Nine of Swords: … this lady brings worry and anxiety, or it could be a woman of this description whom you are worrying over.

Queen of Cups > Six of Pentacles: Kind and thoughtful lady of a gentle nature will be generous to you in some way; may represent a gift or favour, though money is often indicated.

King of Cups

Cups Suit: Emotions. Love and happiness.

Element: Water. Passive. Female energy.

Flow: Gently flowing

Polarity: Neutral

Multiple Kings: Strong male energy, men's group or society, a number of men involved in the situation.

Keywords and Phrases: Kind-hearted and easygoing man.

Applied Meaning

Similar to the Queen, the King of Cups personality types are kind-hearted and easygoing. Cups thrive in warm, loving situations and harmonious surroundings; they are happiest when life is just ticking along nicely. They are considerate and thoughtful and will always try to be helpful to others, a trait that can sometimes be taken advantage of. They can sometimes be soft-hearted when hearing good sob stories, which can make them fall prey to those less well-intentioned.

They rarely make enemies because they're not apt to rock the boat or speak out, even if something upsets them; instead, they'll voice their worry to an indirect source or internalise their frustration. For cups, it is difficult to be assertive or to handle conflict as they don't seem to recognise a middle ground between harmony and aggression. Should a King of Cups lose their temper (which is rare), it may seem out of proportion to the cause, making them appear exasperated and ineffective; such a storm of raging emotions would upset them deeply. They can be masters of avoidance techniques so as to avoid confrontation.

Your King of Cups companion is a pleasure to share time with; they quickly pick up on the vibe if something is amiss with you and you will feel as though no one could understand you better. Loving and supportive, they can provide thoughtful advice and give generously of their time, but don't expect them to fight your battle for you. The King of Cups would rather chew off his right arm than have to deal with something unpleasant!

The King of Cups can be used to represent a man with an astrological water sign: Cancer, Scorpio, or Pisces, which can be useful in email readings.

In career matters they do best in the fields of care-taking, counselling, creative fields, the public sector, nonprofits, charities, humanitarian, or non-competitive environments.

Reversed or Badly Aspected

In the negative, the King of Cups can appear to be childish, sulky, emotionally withholding, an impractical dreamer, melancholy, gullible, weak.

Associations

Supporting or opposing cards don't apply to Kings and Queens as they're neutral and represent people of four distinct personality types.

King of Cups Featured Combinations

A King or Queen can represent the client or someone who will be important to their situation, as indicated by the relevant character description. The extent of the effect they will have and whether it is positive or negative can be seen in the surrounding cards.

King of Cups > Eight of Wands: Good news coming in quickly from a kind and gentle-natured man.

King of Cups > Two of Cups: A deepening relationship with a considerate and romantic man.

Three of Pentacles > King of Cups > Four of Cups: The influence of a gentle-natured and easygoing man connected to your main work leaves you feeling unimpressed.

King of Cups > the High Priestess: A mild-mannered man leads to important information coming to light that will be advantageous for you.

Strength > King of Cups > Nine of Wands: A kind and easygoing man appears to be central to the issue here and is surrounded by a trying situation that may seem like an endurance test. Despite pushing through and soldiering on, you may not feel you are making progress.

ACE OF SWORDS

Swords Suit: Intellect, analytical thought, and challenges.

Suit Element: Air. Active. Male energy.

Flow: Brisk pace

Polarity: Positive

Multiple Aces: Signifies a clean sweep across the board, lots of new beginnings that are linked.

Keywords and Phrases: Triumph over adversity. A fresh start and decisive action.

Applied Meaning

The Ace of Swords is a powerful force when it appears in a reading, indicating that whatever challenges you may be facing can be overcome and you will triumph over adversity. It heralds a fresh start with promising conditions where things are working in your favour, so you can beat the odds even if you feel circumstances are currently stacked against you. I tend to think of this card like the ace up your sleeve.

The Ace is the seed of the suit, the root of power with all the potential that it contains. In order to capitalise upon the favourable aspects that Swords can bring, you will need to use clarity of thought and strength of purpose to act decisively. You are in a position to gain an advantage and come up trumps, so use this power wisely and to the best of your ability.

As with all the Aces, it heralds a new beginning, but you will need to have your wits about you and act with single-minded purpose so as not to miss the wonderful opportunity it presents. This is always a heartening card to see in someone's reading and, in combinations, the perfect placement would often be to close a sequence, to reveal a winning hand and victory for the client. If life has been rife with difficult circumstances, then the Ace of Swords can be like the cavalry appearing over the hill.

Reversed or Badly Aspected

Self-sabotage, defeat with odds stacked against you, muddled thinking, aggressive behaviour.

Associations

Similar and Supporting Cards: The Chariot (triumph over obstacles). Many others reinforce varying aspects, such as: **the Emperor** (taking control), **Strength** (fortitude and courage), **the Hermit** (wisdom), **Justice** (logical and just thought), **the World** (success), **Seven of Wands** (conviction). All **Aces** and **the Fool** would strengthen the aspect of new beginnings.

Opposing and Contradictory Cards: Five of Wands (obstacles), **the Moon** (clouded thinking), **Two of Swords** (indecision), **Eight of Swords** (fear paralysis), **Ten of Swords** (disappointing ending).

Ace of Swords Featured Combinations

Ace of Swords > Ace of Wands: A powerful new beginning, you can overcome challenges to forge ahead and start a new project; pulling the rabbit out of the hat.

Five of Wands > Ace of Swords: Overcoming all obstacles in your path. Winning out over the competition or opposition.

Five of Swords > Ace of Swords: Defeating underhandedness, triumph over those acting dishonourably or trying to discredit you.

Ace of Swords > Four of Pentacles > Four of Swords: You're in a strong position to achieve your aims and are prepared to work hard towards them but overcaution could cause you to step back and the situation could lose momentum.

Five of Pentacles > Ace of Swords: Overcoming a financial problem.

Ace of Swords > Ten of Swords: This is one battle you cannot win and would end in failure; even if you initially triumphed, you would lose in the grand scheme of things—a fleeting victory. Whereas, in the opposite order...

Ten of Swords > Ace of Swords: ... a previous disappointment leaves you undeterred or perhaps more determined because of it. This ending leads to a powerful new beginning and, with the right approach, you have the ability to see it through.

High Priestess > Ace of Swords: Hidden information will be revealed to you and this will help you gain an advantage.

The Lovers > Three of Swords > Temperance > Ace of Swords: Minor quarrels or upheavals in a love relationship can be successfully overcome with patience and a moderate approach; compromise may be called for. Love conquers all, but not without some effort.

The Hermit > Ace of Swords: You're biding your time whilst carefully gathering facts and applying considered thought to the matter before powering forwards with your new plans; getting your ducks in a row.

The Tower > Ace of Swords: Something may fail or fall apart but don't despair, there's a better prize waiting in the wings; you'll need to act calmly and decisively but you can turn this situation around and make a fresh start that will be to your benefit. Whereas, in the opposite order...

Ace of Swords > The Tower: ... your actions could rebound with destructive and far-reaching consequences. A promising new start is anything but; leave this one alone—don't do it.

TWO OF SWORDS

Swords Suit: Intellect, analytical thought, and challenges.

Suit Element: Air. Active. Male energy.

Flow: None

Polarity: Neutral

Multiple Twos: Continuation, development, partnership, balance.

Keywords and Phrases: Stalemate. Indecision. Procrastination.

Applied Meaning

Continuity becomes blocked in the Two of Swords as we find the theme of duality, the flip side where clear thought becomes clouded. The Two of Swords represents a situation that has reached a deadlock—nothing is moving one way or another, creating a stalemate. Sometimes this card can be quite literal to suggest being of two minds over something, so conflicted thoughts and indecision create an impasse, or analysis paralysis. Procrastination can feature, perhaps due to avoidance of an uncomfortable decision.

In relationship matters, the Two of Swords can show something of a stand-off has developed, with neither party prepared to move off the fence or from their respective position. In whichever setting this card appears, it tends to bring matters to a screeching halt, which is most particularly evident at the end of a line when everything leading up to it is moving along at pace, similar to slamming on the brakes or hitting a brick wall (examples follow).

It's not uncommon for people to hope that something external will release the situation for them, but the metaphorical blindfold needs to be removed in order to gain clarity. To break the existing gridlock, something will need to happen: a decision must be made or an action must be taken.

In combinations, you can quite often find both the Hanged Man and the Two of Swords present in the reading to reinforce one another, showing matters that appear to be progressing coming to a standstill. Your interest would be in the card following to see how or if it will be broken.

Reversed or Badly Aspected

Can represent duplicity or disloyalty. Refusal to see; being in denial.

Associations

> **Similar and Supporting Cards: The Hanged Man** (suspension), **the Moon** (uncertainty), **Eight of Swords** (restriction), the **Seven of Cups** (choices) to some extent and from a place of indecision.
>
> **Opposing and Contradictory Cards: Justice** (balanced thought and logic), **the Magician** (proactive), **the Emperor** (leadership), **the Chariot** (exerting your will). In terms of speed, any fast-moving card.

Two of Swords Featured Combinations

Three of Wands > Two of Swords: Early accomplishments could hit a stumbling block; gridlock delays the next steps. Progress in trade or commerce stalls.

Eight of Wands > the Chariot > Two of Swords: The brick wall scenario where everything racing along comes to a halt. Can also indicate a holdup with travel plans (travel combination and overlap meaning in the first two cards).

Ace of Cups > Two of Swords > Two of Cups > the Hanged Man: A new relationship appears to be blowing hot and cold, stop and start; external conditions could be the cause but may lead to you reassessing this connection.

Two of Swords > Seven of Cups > the Hanged Man: Nothing is progressing here, and you're going in circles contemplating differing scenarios without a resolution. Dithering and indecision create a logjam—complete reassessment required. Whereas...

Seven of Cups > Two of Swords: ... this is the feeling of being blindsided by too many options and possibilities. Narrow your choices or you may be left without any.

Knight of Cups > Two of Swords: An offer may leave you undecided. Alternatively, there may be a pause before matters can be taken forwards (surrounding cards would clarify).

Two of Swords > Knight of Swords: Nothing happens and then it all happens at once.

Two of Swords > Two of Pentacles: You may be purposely maintaining the status quo in a situation. Alternatively, some jiggling and careful attention can get a stalled situation moving.

Two of Swords > Four of Pentacles: You have serious misgivings about moving forwards and indecision can lead to caution as to whether to proceed at all. If the stalemate didn't originate through your own design, you'll be reaching a stage where you want to step further back from the matter.

Two of Swords > the Emperor: The pause may be only temporary, but you'll be prepared to grasp the nettle and do what needs to be done; seize the moment and take control.

The Lovers > Three of Swords > Two of Swords: This may have started as a lovers' tiff but could lead to a standoff; someone needs to make the first move to stop matters becoming entrenched.

Two of Swords > the Hermit: You're not prepared to be rushed but will give the matter deep consideration whilst looking into it further. There can be a tendency to turn inward, but it holds the potential to find the answer you are seeking.

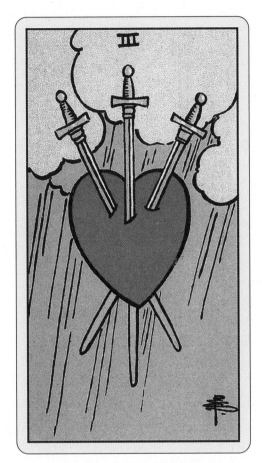

THREE OF SWORDS

Swords Suit: Intellect, analytical thought, and challenges.

Suit Element: Air. Active. Male energy.

Flow: Turbulent, choppy

Polarity: Negative

Multiple Threes: Progress and expansion.

Keywords and Phrases: Upsets and quarrels. Upheaval.
Stormy emotions. Separation through distance
(long-distance relationship).

Applied Meaning

As the image suggests, the Three of Swords can bring cutting words, spiky exchanges, and emotional upset. In simple lines, and depending upon surrounding cards, this card often reveals minor quarrels, bickering, upsets, or upheavals in family situations.

As a low number, it tends to be more inclined towards minor disagreements, divided opinions, squabbling, or harsh words said in haste *unless* it is surrounded and supported by more negative cards, which then suggests a more serious tone or downturn in events. Oftentimes, when suggesting minor disagreements, you can see by the cards following that the situation doesn't gather momentum and it can look out of place. As always, the last card following has the final say, but I would usually look for the Ten of Swords or Death for evidence of an ending and parting of ways.

As an outcome card in a positional spread or in answer to a set question, it is probably not the card we wish to see, as the traditional meaning is one of heartbreak and sorrow, but as previously mentioned in the first section of the book, the card will respond to the meaning you have decided and placed upon it.

If this card appears in the relationship area of the Life Spread, I have found it can often indicate a long-distance relationship, or one where the couple are separated due to life circumstances, rather than a split or parting of ways, unless surrounding cards state otherwise.

Reversed or Badly Aspected

Disorder and disruption, incompatibility, confusion, outside interference, denial.

Associations

Similar and Supporting Cards: Five of Wands (differences), **Five of Cups** (sorrow and tears), **Nine of Swords** (worry and anxiety).

Opposing and Contradictory Cards: Temperance (harmony and balance), **Three of Cups** (group celebrations), **Ten of Cups** (happy heart).

Three of Swords Featured Combinations

Two of Wands > Three of Swords: Quarrels and upheavals in a working partnership, an uncomfortable working relationship. Similarly...

Three of Pentacles > Three of Swords: ... disagreements and upsets at work.

King of Wands > Three of Swords > King of Pentacles: An argument that affects the client originates from an outgoing and confident man who can be impetuous (his card being first shows he brings the argument into play); what happens next will be dependent upon the action or behaviour of a steady and reliable man. (Unless your client is one of these men, it usually shows their involvement rather than a disagreement between the two Kings, as we're reading a progression of events.)

Three of Swords > Two of Cups: A long-distance relationship.

Three of Swords > Knight of Pentacles > the Tower > Death: A long-standing quarrel, or one that's been festering for a while over an old issue, finally erupts, which will bring a definite end to the matter with the person/people in question.

Five of Swords > High Priestess > Three of Swords: A hidden deceit, or something dishonest occurring in the background, will be revealed and brought to your attention, which results in a disagreement. Whereas ...

Three of Swords > Five of Swords: ... if this quarrel escalates, it could turn nasty. Better to let this one go as no one wins and the other party could become vengeful.

Five of Pentacles > Three of Swords: Argument over a financial shortfall or an unexpected bill/expense. Quarrelling over money issues.

Ten of Pentacles > Three of Swords > Temperance: Upsets with family members, but patient handling can bring healing and resolution, although it may take some time. Could also represent a dispute with a property matter that would bring upheavals in a family situation; the matter can be settled amicably with diplomacy and compromise.

The Lovers > Three of Swords > Ten of Swords: Arguments or upset in a love relationship leads to a disappointing ending.

Judgement > Three of Swords: An issue that refuses to die, an old argument resurrected and brought back round again. Whereas in the opposite order ...

Three of Swords > Judgement: ... the indication is reconciliation after an argument.

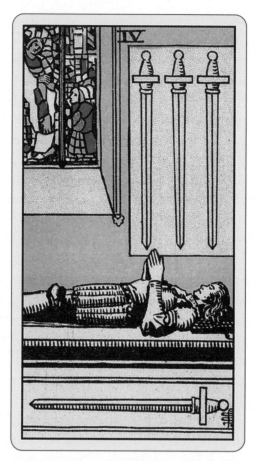

Four of Swords

Swords Suit: Intellect, analytical thought, and challenges.

Suit Element: Air. Active. Male energy.

Flow: Pause

Polarity: Positive/Neutral

Multiple Fours: Structure and stability.

Keywords and Phrases: Rest and recovery, recuperation. Consolidation. Withdrawal.

Applied Meaning

The Four of Swords represents rest and recovery following stresses or strains. Time is needed to rejuvenate and replenish energy levels before resuming. It can bring an air of detachment to outside events, one where you may just feel the need to pull back and withdraw momentarily; it is a pause rather than a full stop for some quiet time to stop and smell the roses.

In relationship situations, it can indicate pulling back or a time-out (perhaps following a difficult situation), suggesting retreat and time for each party to take a breath or lick their wounds; to allow things to calm down after heated moments to stop matters getting out of hand. Sometimes it can simply show that someone has stepped back or withdrawn from the relationship, which may only be a temporary measure although not an ideal indication if someone is hoping to see progress.

For business affairs, this card can represent consolidation or pulling together available resources to strengthen or stabilise a position. It may also indicate a fallow period when the order books are quiet.

Finally, the card may show a period of convalescence, recuperation, and restoration following an illness or a stay in hospital.

Reversed or Badly Aspected

Activity has resumed but is advancing slowly; a cautious approach.

Associations

Similar and Supporting Cards: Six of Swords (moving into calmer times), **the Hermit** (solitude), **the Star** and **Temperance** (healing aspect), **Strength** (inner reserves of strength).

Opposing and Contradictory Cards: Three of Cups (socialising), **the Sun** (happiness and vitality), **Eight of Wands** (swift movement), **the Chariot** (exerting will, pushing forwards).

Four of Swords Featured Combinations

Four of Swords > Ace of Wands: Can represent an incubation period prior to starting a new project.

Three of Wands > Four of Swords: There could be a need to take a breather following progress before moving on again; pulling back slightly to firm up existing position, pausing expansion.

Ace of Cups > Four of Swords > the Hanged Man: Pulling back in a new relationship, maybe having second thoughts and reassessing but no movement going forwards.

Five of Cups > Four of Swords: Rest and recovery following an emotional upset.

Four of Swords > Ace of Swords: Recovery to advance in a stronger position.

Three of Swords > Four of Swords: Stepping back from the fray, taking time out and withdrawing following squabbles or conflict.

Three of Pentacles > Ten of Wands > Four of Swords: Taking time out after pressure at work; be careful of overworking and burnout.

Four of Swords > Four of Pentacles: Consolidating finances and material concerns, replenishing stock and exercising caution with what you have. Similarly…

Five of Pentacles > Four of Swords > Four of Pentacles: …shows pulling together resources and reserves to recover from a financial setback.

High Priestess > Four of Swords > the Hermit: Meditation retreat or spiritual sanctuary.

The Hierophant > Four of Swords: Can indicate a hospital stay. Similarly…

The Hierophant > Four of Swords > Temperance: …indicates recovery and healing following a hospital stay, convalescence. The Star instead of Temperance adds assurance for improvement to health matters.

The Devil > Four of Swords: Pulling back to recover from a toxic or unhealthy situation. Alternatively, can indicate addiction rehabilitation or a recovery programme.

FIVE OF SWORDS

Swords Suit: Intellect, analytical thought, and challenges.

Suit Element: Air. Active. Male energy.

Flow: Unstable; an ill wind

Polarity: Negative

Multiple Fives: Challenges and instability.

Keywords and Phrases: Underhandedness. Hidden agenda.
Malice. Hollow victory by unfair means.

Applied Meaning

The Five of Swords is never a pleasant visitor in a reading; it can suggest unscrupulous people using unfair tactics to get what they want regardless of the cost. It can represent hostility, spiteful behaviour, or malicious gossip intended to harm your reputation or undermine you to gain an upper hand. I tend to think of this card as a bit of a thug as it can show aggression and bullying in some form, although it is heightened and takes a more serious tone when accompanied by the Devil.

This card can act as a warning to underhandedness going on around you and can suggest an aspect of secrecy with a hidden agenda, so someone may be acting in a deceitful and dishonest manner. It can sometimes indicate theft but usually shows someone trying to take advantage using selfish and unfair means, where your loss would be to their gain and there are no holds barred or scruples in order to win at any price.

On a personal level, this card reminds you to check your own motives in a situation before proceeding, as it can lead to a hollow victory where unethical actions can come back to bite you once uncovered, bringing a sense of shame. Confrontations should be avoided; no one wins the battle with the Five of Swords. Any victory is temporary and ultimately leads to humiliation and defeat.

On a more positive note, the benefit of this card is that if it appears in a future position, it provides advance warning of where the problem may lie. Remember that this card is a Five, so the nature is unstable but temporary, so with the right approach you should be able to avert the situation.

Reversed or Badly Aspected

The meaning remains relatively unchanged but intensified.

Associations

>   **Similar and Supporting Cards:** Differing aspects of secrecy can be found with **the Devil** and **the Moon** and they often appear together to reinforce one another. **Seven of Swords** (stealth, theft), **the Devil** (toxic).
>
>   **Opposing and Contradictory Cards: Ace of Swords** (triumph over adversity); the **High Priestess** has a secrecy aspect but usually of a beneficial nature. **The Chariot** (victory over challenges), **the Hierophant** (morals and doing the right thing), **Justice** (fair and balanced).

Five of Swords Featured Combinations

Three of Wands > Five of Swords: Can be counterfeit goods, dishonest commercial or trade dealings; possible trading theft.

Five of Wands > Five of Swords: A conflict of interests may be used dishonestly. Petty rivalry could take a more serious turn, or the competition could be setting you up. (Two Fives also highlight the instability of the situation).

Eight of Wands > Five of Swords: Online bullying or trolling can be indicated. Poison pen letter. Libel. Information in this message can't be trusted and holds an ulterior motive. Also …

Five of Swords > the Moon > Seven of Swords: … hidden adversaries, anonymous trolling or sniping from behind the scenes intended to cause harm and damage your reputation—handle with care.

Three of Cups > Five of Swords: False friends who do not have your best interests at heart—be careful. Malicious gossip-mongering from a social group.

Three of Pentacles > Five of Swords: Professional jealousy; watch your back regarding hostility and internal politics. May indicate workplace bullying.

Five of Swords > Five of Pentacles: Financial theft or scam, can also apply in the opposite order. If the Devil is also present …

The Devil > Five of Swords > Five of Pentacles: … can add more serious nefarious overtones, such as criminal activities.

Any Page > Five of Swords > Nine of Swords: Can reveal a bullying issue causing anxiety and concern surrounding a child—the page's suit would indicate the child's personality. The Page could also be in the central position.

Any King or Queen > Five of Swords: One of the Kings or Queens preceding the Five of Swords would identify the person by description of where the problem is coming from; someone not to be trusted.

Five of Swords > Justice: Justice prevails, unless surrounded by further supporting indications such as the following two combinations:

Justice > Five of Swords > the Devil: May show perverting the course of justice, dirty tricks and corrupt activity in a legal matter. Also …

Justice > Five of Swords: ... fraudulent legal papers, shady dealings hidden in a contract; don't sign it. An injustice through dishonesty, perjury, lying under oath.

The Moon > the Lovers > Five of Swords: Dishonesty surrounding a relationship; someone is not telling you the truth and can't be trusted; hidden agenda.

SIX OF SWORDS

Swords Suit: Intellect, analytical thought, and challenges.

Suit Element: Air. Active. Male energy.

Flow: Slower pace

Polarity: Positive

Multiple Sixes: Harmony and improvement.

Keywords and Phrases: Moving into calmer times. Travel (journey over water).

Applied Meaning

The Six of Swords is one of the more promising cards in the Swords suit, along with the Ace and the Four. Whatever difficulties you may have experienced, this card indicates turning a corner and heading into a more peaceful phase. It suggests the calm after the storm—moving from stormy waters into calmer times, as shown by the difference in the choppy waves to the near side of the boat and the clear stretch ahead on the other.

Although problems are being left behind, the six Swords in the boat indicates that the wisdom gained through the experience stays with you—perhaps as the wisdom of hindsight—and suggests clarity in overcoming emotional turmoil or turbulent times. If there are difficult or stressful cards, look for the Six of Swords to show recovery from the situation.

The Six of Swords is also one of the travel cards and can sometimes represent a journey over water. If other cards representing travel are also present, it will highlight that aspect. When followed by a challenging card, it can be a warning to be careful that you don't move away from one problem straight into another (example follow). In some instances it can be more literal, to represent leaving a situation and moving on.

Reversed or Badly Aspected

Postponement; difficulties remain unresolved.

Associations

> **Similar and Supporting Cards: Four of Swords** (recovery after strain), **Temperance** (harmony and healing), **the Star** (brighter times). Other cards representing travel reinforce this aspect: **the Chariot**, **Eight of Wands**, **Knight of Wands**.
>
> **Opposing and Contradictory Cards: Five of Wands** (friction), **Ten of Wands** (burdens), **Eight of Swords** (restriction), **Nine of Swords** (worry), **the Tower** (disruption).

Six of Swords Featured Combinations

Three of Wands > Six of Swords: Merchant shipping and trade cargo, import and export. Progress brings a clear stretch ahead.

Five of Wands > Two of Cups > Six of Swords: Release from tensions in a close relationship; friction will ease and calm will be restored.

Eight of Wands > the World > Six of Swords: International travel, can be world cruise (reinforced travel meaning). Alternatively, triumphant news leads to freedom from previous problems.

Ten of Wands > Six of Swords: A burden released and moving on from problems; the situation will improve and life will enter a more peaceful phase. Whereas...

Ten of Wands > Six of Swords > the Tower: ...a brief respite, but check your bearings to avoid drifting into a more difficult situation.

Eight of Cups > Six of Swords: You may finally decide to walk away from a trying situation, but life will start to improve as a result.

Six of Swords > Four of Swords: Taking a trip for rest and recovery, respite care, or convalescence. Whereas...

Four of Swords > Six of Swords: ...pulling back from a situation will be beneficial and lead to improvement.

Knight of Swords > Six of Swords: A period of calm after frenzied activity, calm after chaos. A journey made in haste, last-minute travel.

Wheel of Fortune > Six of Swords: A definite change towards more favourable conditions leading to a peaceful period on the horizon.

Death > Six of Swords: Moving on following a major transition in life.

Six of Swords > the Star: Smooth progression of events to show a period of healing and life gradually improving and getting brighter over time.

SEVEN OF SWORDS

Swords Suit: Intellect, analytical thought, and challenges.

Suit Element: Air. Active. Male energy.

Flow: Crosswinds

Polarity: Neutral/Negative

Multiple Sevens: A cycle change.

Keywords and Phrases: Stealth and strategy. A cunning plan! Theft.

Applied Meaning

The Seven of Swords can act as a warning to handle something with extreme care, whether this may be a person or a delicate situation. You will need to have your wits about you and formulate a well-considered strategy that requires careful manoeuvring. Do not be tempted to overplay your hand. In the Golden Dawn tradition, this card is known as "Lord of Unstable Effort" and suggests only partial success, often due to an ill-conceived plan or lack of effort and commitment.

As a card of stealth it can highlight questionable activities, as it suggests someone tiptoeing around behind the scenes. However, in combination with the Page of Swords, it can indicate surveillance and undercover work, whether for good or ill, depending upon how it is influenced by surrounding cards. This particular combination in readings as a representation of surveillance matters is more widespread nowadays, as undercover work is more commonplace than it used to be, e.g., police, military, tax office, or financial investigations. It tends to be more commonly found in those settings rather than the popular view of spying and intelligence services, although that may depend upon the type of people you read for! In larger spreads, other secrecy cards are usually also evident, most particularly the Moon.

Due to the image, some see this as a card of theft, although I prefer the Five of Swords to indicate unscrupulous behaviour; as a pair, they could reinforce this aspect. If the Seven of Swords appears in the final outcome position of a spread, it can sometimes indicate an unexpected twist; events may not turn out quite as planned or are only partially successful.

Reversed or Badly Aspected

Taking good advice and acting upon it. Secret plans uncovered; being caught red-handed.

Associations

Similar and Supporting Cards: Five of Swords (secrecy, theft), **the Moon** (secrecy, illusion), **the Devil** (secrecy, corruption), **Page of Swords** (spying, undercover), **Four of Pentacles**, and **the Hermit** (caution).

Opposing and Contradictory Cards: The High Priestess (secrets revealed). **Justice** (balanced thought), **Seven of Pentacles** (careful preparation).

Seven of Swords Featured Combinations

Five of Swords > Seven of Swords: Reinforces the indication of theft.

Seven of Swords > the High Priestess: Plans may not be as secret as supposed; a secret plan uncovered and exposed. Also ...

Seven of Swords > Page of Swords > the High Priestess: ... with the Seven and Page in this order, it can show a whistle-blower or anonymous tip-off that leads to a secret plan being revealed.

Seven of Swords > the Chariot > the Tower: Fools rush in where angels fear to tread! Going from one extreme to another leads to failure.

Seven of Swords > the Lovers > the Devil: Secret assignations, may suggest a clandestine relationship (but check other indications in the spread as well).

Seven of Swords > the Hermit: Extreme care is indicated from the shared and reinforced meaning; do your homework, gather all the facts, think things through in careful detail, and proceed cautiously.

Seven of Swords > the Devil: May suggest stalking. Sneaking around for negative purposes.

Temperance > Seven of Wands > Seven of Swords: Cautious strategy applied with patience and diplomacy leads to partially successful negotiations; compromises will be required, as you won't receive everything you hoped for.

Page of Swords > Seven of Swords: Highlights surveillance or undercover activities. *A preceding card can help provide more detail and indication for the setting, such as in:*

Three of Wands > Page of Swords > Seven of Swords: Commercial espionage.

Justice > Page of Swords > Seven of Swords: Police undercover and surveillance work.

King or Queen of Swords > Page of Swords > Seven of Swords: Military surveillance and/or covert special operations.

The Magician > Page of Swords > Seven of Swords: Private investigators, professional snoop; agent.

The Hierophant > Page of Swords > Seven of Swords: Government departments, i.e., tax office, or benefits investigations.

The Emperor > Page of Swords > Seven of Swords: Intelligence agencies.

EIGHT OF SWORDS

Swords Suit: Intellect, analytical thought, and challenges.

Suit Element: Air. Active. Male energy.

Flow: Stalling, choppy

Polarity: Negative

Multiple Eights: Flow and movement.

Keywords and Phrases: Limitation and restriction. Feeling trapped.

Applied Meaning

The Eight of Swords can indicate a situation where you feel trapped by fearful thoughts; things seem outside of your control or you feel powerless to change anything. It can create paralysis in the prison of your mind, as the mental monsters go round in a circle, holding you captive to them.

Swords reflect the double-edged nature of the suit, so just as fears can make you feel hemmed in, they may also suggest the power of clarity can release you through illuminated thought. A calm head is needed to look at the problem in order to recognise the truth of the matter and reveal a solution so you can release yourself and break the cycle. There is usually a way out of the matter, although it could feel uncomfortable, which in itself can lead to avoidance that perpetuates the cycle.

Aside from the psychological aspects of this card, it can often reveal a very real and physical restriction that affects a person's lifestyle in some way, so it's not always limited to fearful thought processes. As always, a sensitive approach is recommended. For example, I've found this card in settings of those caring for a disabled child or relative, or for people who are housebound, which has added constraints and a certain level of confinement to what would be considered normal everyday life and activities. Further examples are provided here.

In simple lines, look at the card immediately before the Eight of Swords to see what creates the limitation and the cards following to see if and how it can be released.

Reversed or Badly Aspected

Breaking the cycle, removal of obstacles, releasing constraints and breaking free. If badly aspected, can intensify the situation.

Associations

> **Similar and Supporting Cards: Two of Swords** (stalemate), **the Hanged Man** (suspension), **Nine of Swords** (anxiety), **Ten of Wands,** and **the Devil** (weighed down).
>
> **Opposing and Contradictory Cards: Ace of Swords** (clarity of thought), **Knight of Swords** (decisive action), **the Magician** (confidence and initiative), **Justice** (balanced thought), **the Emperor** (rationale), **the Chariot** (focused thought and exerting will).

Eight of Swords Featured Combinations

Two of Wands > Eight of Swords: Limitations within a joint venture, may feel trapped within the arrangement.

Ten of Wands > Eight of Swords: Feeling trapped or restricted by too many responsibilities, too much going on but feel powerless to change it.

Six of Cups > Eight of Swords: Trapped in the past; a past situation or memories that you feel unable to move beyond.

Seven of Cups > Eight of Swords: Surrounded by options but unable to make a decision therefore keeping you locked in a cycle.

Eight of Swords > Ace of Swords: A breakthrough; despite the odds, you will overcome whatever challenges have been causing the limitations, through clarity of thought and determined action.

Eight of Swords > Nine of Swords: Progression of events, leads to more worry over the initial concerns. Anxiety could be creating a holding pattern and help may be needed to make progress. Also...

Nine of Swords > Eight of Swords: ...can represent debilitating anxiety.

Three of Pentacles > Eight of Swords: Feeling restricted within your role at work or the sense of a dead-end job, possibly the limitations of a glass-ceiling situation, particularly if the Hanged Man follows.

Five of Pentacles > Eight of Swords: Locked into debt or a financial problem that you feel unable to solve. An unexpected bill could leave you in a fix. Poverty trap. Can sometimes indicate limitations through a lack mentality or scarcity mindset.

The Hierophant > Eight of Swords > Four of Swords: Can indicate hospital confinement, convalescence, and recovery after hospital stay. Whereas...

The Hierophant >the Emperor > Justice > Eight of Swords: ...may suggest the confinement of being detained at His Majesty's Pleasure—prison! (Derives from British slang.) Can appear in any order, sometimes with the Eight of Swords central and surrounded by these three majors. May also just appear as **Eight of Swords > the Devil:** Detainment or imprisonment, which can also apply to other settings.

Judgement > Eight of Swords: A recurring cycle, resurrection of an old situation that you feel locked into and unable to release from.

NINE OF SWORDS

Swords Suit: Intellect, analytical thought, and challenges.

Suit Element: Air. Active. Male energy.

Flow: Stalling, choppy

Polarity: Negative

Multiple Nines: Tying up loose ends, penultimate number.

Keywords and Phrases: Worry and anxiety. Mental anguish.

Applied Meaning

As the penultimate number for the suit of challenges, the Nine of Swords reaches the pinnacle before completion in the Ten. If left unchecked, the debilitating concerns found in the Eight progress to a high level of worry and anxiety.

Sitting upright in bed, a despairing figure covers their face with their hands and appears to be experiencing a dark night of the soul as nine Swords dominate the darkness and bleak backdrop of the scene. Similarly, we tend to worry when we can't see a solution to a problem, creating sleepless nights and all-encompassing worry that overshadows all else. The message of this card can act as a reminder of the double-edged nature of Swords, of challenges or clarity that can cut both ways. If we can face our worst fears, we may find the wisdom contained therein to conquer them.

In simple lines, look to the preceding card to see what initiated the anxiety; obviously, we hope to find the situation clearing as we move forwards after the Nine. One thing to check with this card is to see if the other stress cards are present anywhere else in the spread, which will add more weight to the situation overall. If this card appears alone (and particularly when surrounded by favourable cards), it can suggest unnecessarily worrying and sometimes impostor syndrome (as shown in the following sections).

Reversed or Badly Aspected

Can indicate the start of recovery, damaging gossip, though some consider this reversal as additional struggles.

Associations

> **Similar and Supporting Cards: Ten of Wands** and **the Devil** (heavy burden), **Five of Cups** (sadness and regret), **Eight of Swords** (trapped by fear).
>
> Collectively, watch for accompanying cards that can reinforce stressful conditions, such as: **Eight of Swords, Nine of Swords, Nine of Wands, Ten of Wands, the Devil.**
>
> **Opposing and Contradictory Cards: The Star** (hope and optimism), **Temperance** (balanced emotions), **Three of Cups** (joy), **the Sun** (happiness).

Nine of Swords Featured Combinations

Ace of Wands > Nine of Swords: Worrying over a new job or project; a new business or venture brings sleepless nights (check following cards to see if this lifts).

Three of Wands > Nine of Swords: Commercial or trading concerns; progress and expansion also bring worries.

Eight of Wands > Nine of Swords: Sudden news that causes concern; worrying news.

Nine of Swords > Eight of Cups: Leaving worries behind; this may not be a decision taken lightly, but you will finally decide to walk away from the situation causing concern.

Five of Pentacles > Nine of Swords: Money worries.

Ten of Pentacles > Nine of Swords: Family worries; could be concerns relating to a property matter.

The Lovers > Nine of Swords: Relationship angst.

Nine of Swords > Strength > Six of Wands: "Feel the fear and do it anyway!" If you can keep going and work through your anxieties, you will find support and encouragement and can win the day.

The Hermit > Nine of Swords: Could become isolated due to fears. Whereas, in the opposite order…

Nine of Swords > the Hermit: … taking time to think things through and collect helpful information. An older person or someone wiser through experience may be able to offer advice to alleviate your fears.

Nine of Swords > Temperance: May be an indication of therapy or counselling services to help restore harmony and balance. (The addition of **the Hierophant** could add formal institutions, such as hospitals.)

The Moon > Nine of Swords > the Devil: Worries can take a more serious turn when surrounded by these two cards: the Moon can alter perception of reality and the Devil adds weight with the potential of an unhealthy situation developing. It may be time to seek outside help.

The World > Nine of Swords > the Sun: Unfounded fears and unnecessary worry anticipating the worst. If appearing in connection to work-related matters it may suggest suffering from impostor syndrome.

TEN OF SWORDS

Swords Suit: Intellect, analytical thought, and challenges.

Suit Element: Air. Active. Male energy.

Flow: Stop

Polarity: Negative

Multiple Tens: Completion of a cycle.

Keywords and Phrases: Disappointing ending. Failed plans.

Applied Meaning

As completion of the suit, the Ten of Swords brings an ending usually felt with an air of disappointment or defeat. Sometimes things just don't work out, leaving a sense of failure to your plans; an event you were looking forwards to is cancelled, or projects fall through. The Ten brings the completion of challenges and in certain circumstances can represent the ending of a difficult situation, which may be welcomed—now you can move on.

As a reader, it can be tempting to try to dress up less favourable cards; no one wishes to deliver bad news. However, not everything in life is destined to succeed or bring the happy outcome we hope for or envisage. In future positions, the Ten of Swords provides forewarning and can help prevent wasted time, effort, money, or emotions on something that could fail to live up to expectations. This then provides an opportunity to consider other avenues that may be available.

The Ten of Swords brings an ending and closure to the cycle, but if you're looking for new beginnings, check further ahead in the spread to see if and when the Aces arrive to start a new cycle.

Reversed or Badly Aspected

A temporary respite when you can find an advantage to help your situation. Possibility of improvement and relief. When badly aspected, it accentuates the negative.

Associations

Similar and Supporting Cards: Death (final ending), **the Tower** (collapse, though usually more unexpected).

Opposing and Contradictory Cards: The Sun (happiness), **the World** (success), **Aces** or **the Fool** (new beginnings).

Ten of Swords Featured Combinations

Ace of Wands > Ten of Swords: Things may not work out as you hoped. Despite the excitement, a new endeavour could fizzle out quickly and end in disappointment.

Nine of Wands > Ten of Swords: Despite your best efforts, success is not indicated; it may be better to cut your losses.

Knight of Wands > Ten of Swords: House move falls through.

Three of Cups > Ten of Swords: Cancelled social event, plans fall through. Alternatively, a disappointing ending comes about following (and possibly due to) the social event.

Knight of Cups > Eight of Pentacles > Ten of Swords: A work offer may be withdrawn or revoked; even if it progresses at first, it will not last long.

Three of Swords > Ten of Swords: An escalating problem or serious quarrel that leads to separation and brings matters to a close.

Ten of Swords > Six of Swords: Life will begin to improve following the ending of a difficult situation.

Knight of Pentacles > Ten of Swords: A long-standing or long-awaited situation finally comes to a close and this may not be the result you were hoping for.

The Fool > Ten of Swords: Look before you leap—you could be rushing headlong into a situation where you lack experience or one that is beyond your comfort zone that ends in disappointment; a new opportunity may not be all you thought it to be and leads to failure; something is over almost before it has begun.

Justice > Ten of Swords: Legal contract rescinded, disappointment of swift end to a contract. Defeated in a legal matter.

Ten of Swords > the Sun: "Every cloud has a silver lining"; a turnaround situation that may feel disappointing at first but could bring a blessing in disguise.

The World > Ten of Swords: Limited or short-lived success; seek alternative plans for the longer term.

Page of Swords

Swords Suit: Intellect, analytical thought, and challenges.

Suit Element: Air. Active. Male energy.

Flow: Pause

Polarity: Negative/Neutral

Multiple Pages: Multiple messages, children's group.

Keywords and Phrases: Delayed news and setbacks. A serious child.

Applied Meaning

As the Pages represent messages arriving, the Page of Swords indicates a delay to news you may be waiting for. It can also signal news that is slightly disappointing; since the Page is depicted as a child, it makes it easy to remember as disappointing news of a *minor* nature—not *quite* what you were hoping to hear, but not usually more serious than that. Primarily, it tends to suggest delayed news and setbacks.

When describing the personality of a minor, the Page of Swords is the old head on young shoulders; they appear more mature than their years and usually take responsibilities seriously. All Sword characters have good mental agility and capacity, so their curious and inquisitive nature thrives on information and mental stimulation. They may appear to have a serious demeanour but it is usually because they are distracted by their thought processes, making them appear distant or aloof. They like to see fair play and are naturally analytical; as deep thinkers, they can sometimes astound you with profound questions with a philosophical bent. The Sword child is on a constant quest to ascertain "why?"

An unusual aspect of this card is that when it appears alongside the Seven of Swords, it can indicate surveillance and undercover activities or spying. More information about this aspect appears under the Seven of Swords on page 128.

Reversed or Badly Aspected

Can suggest problems surrounding a child. In the right combinations, it can indicate undercover activities, surveillance, spying, a whistle-blower, gossip, or troublemakers.

Associations

Similar and Supporting Cards: Two of Swords or the Hanged Man (delays), Seven of Swords (spying), Five of Swords (gossip).

Opposing and Contradictory Cards: Six of Wands (bearer of great news), Eight of Wands (good news coming in quickly), Knight of Swords (speed), the other Pages (good news, as relevant to the suit).

Page of Swords Featured Combinations

Eight of Wands > Page of Swords: News will arrive quickly but brings a minor disappointment.

Knight of Wands > Page of Swords: Setbacks concerning a house move.

Page of Swords > Eight of Cups: News may not be what you were hoping for, but it's time to close the door and turn your attention in a different direction.

Page of Swords > Knight of Cups: The offer or invitation may be delayed, but it will come through.

Seven of Pentacles > Page of Swords: If you're waiting for a payment, it will be slightly delayed; arrange a contingency plan.

Page of Swords > Eight of Pentacles: Could be a delayed start to new work, or news concerning a new job is held up. Whereas, in the opposite order...

Eight of Pentacles > Page of Swords: ... disappointing news concerning new work.

Page of Swords > Knight of Pentacles: Delayed information finally arrives—you may have been waiting for this news for quite some time.

Page of Swords > Three of Swords: Disappointing news that causes a rift.

Page of Swords > Knight of Swords: News may be delayed, but be prepared to move swiftly once it arrives as it could become quite chaotic.

Page of Swords > High Priestess: News received may not be quite what you hope to hear, but don't dismiss it too quickly, as it also contains hidden information coming to light which will now be to your advantage. Also watch for...

Seven of Swords > Page of Swords > the High Priestess: ... as it can be undercover activities revealed; may involve a whistle-blower or anonymous tip-off.

KNIGHT OF SWORDS

Swords Suit: Intellect, analytical thought, and challenges.

Suit Element: Air. Active. Male energy.

Flow: Fast, whirlwind.

Polarity: Positive

Multiple Knights: Lots of movement and plenty of action.

Keywords and Phrases: Chaotic speed and decisive action.

Applied Meaning

The Knight of Swords brings an enormous amount of speed with a sense of urgency into the equation: you may be hotfooting it and events could feel quite hectic, but it certainly gets things moving.

When this card makes an appearance, it brings a powerful force charging into play with all the subtlety of a whirlwind and the resulting chaos that surrounds it. It therefore suggests the need to be ready to move quickly and act decisively in order to stay abreast of events and take full advantage of the situation.

It's not unusual to see the Knight of Swords accompanied by the Eight of Wands somewhere in the spread, as if re-emphasising the overlap in meaning. The Knight often appears after hold-ups, similar to the effect of a cork suddenly exploding out of a bottle with pent-up energy.

The speedy nature of the card can be helpful with regard to timing; when preceding other cards, it shows that the events described by the following cards will unfold rapidly, and in the starting or present position it can be almost immediate. If the Knight of Swords appears at the end of a simple line or for the future outcome, it shows the situation will pick up pace, adding a sense of urgency once matters reach that stage.

Reversed or Badly Aspected

Aggressively rushing headlong into a situation with a lack of good judgement; antagonistic tendencies; rash behavior, a lack of discretion.

Associations

Similar and Supporting Cards: Eight of Wands (swift movement), **the Chariot** (powerful force of energy driving forwards).

Opposing and Contradictory Cards: Knight of Pentacles (slow and steady by comparison), **Two of Swords, the Hanged Man** (no movement).

Knight of Swords Featured Combinations

Knight of Swords > Ace of Wands: Hitting the ground running; a sense of urgency and a new venture set in motion with great speed and decisive action.

Three of Wands > Seven of Wands > Knight of Swords: Trade and commercial negotiations could be tough but should result in swift progression and expansion of plans.

Ace of Cups > Knight of Swords > Ten of Cups: A whirlwind romance; a new relationship that quickly becomes serious.

Knight of Swords > Three of Cups: A last-minute social event.

Knight of Swords > Knight of Cups: Sudden proposal, invitation, or offer—a card preceding the Knight of Swords would identify the nature of the proposal.

Knight of Swords > Two of Pentacles: Will need to have your wits about you to keep everything flowing smoothly, as events will seem to be happening at warp speed; things could require some frantic juggling with multiple situations.

Seven of Pentacles > Knight of Swords: Fast return on investments.

Knight of Swords > Wheel of Fortune: "Life can turn on a sixpence." Swift change in circumstances (should be fortunate unless followed by a negative card).

Justice > Knight of Swords > the World: Quick and decisive action concerning a legal matter brings a triumphant conclusion.

Knight of Swords > Death: Sudden and swift closure to a matter. Racing for the deadline.

Knight of Swords > the Hanged Man: Similar to running straight into a brick wall; speed comes to nought as everything falls into a holding pattern (similar with the **Two of Swords**). Whereas, in the opposite order ...

The Hanged Man > Knight of Swords: ... can bring relief as situations suddenly spring into action after hold-ups.

QUEEN OF SWORDS

Swords Suit: Intellect, analytical thought, and challenges.

Suit Element: Air. Active. Male energy.

Flow: Brisk

Polarity: Neutral

Multiple Queens: A group of women, women's society.

Keywords and Phrases: Perceptive and independent lady. Seeker of truth.

Applied Meaning

In traditional decks back in the day, the Queen of Swords received a bad rap and was considered an embittered lady of misfortune: unmarried, childless, divorced, or widowed in an age when it was considered a most unfortunate state of affairs for a woman's status and circumstances. Thankfully, views have changed in modern times!

The Queen of Swords is an independent woman who knows her own mind, regardless of relationship status. She is observant and perceptive with a sharp and agile mind that doesn't tend to miss anything because she is naturally analytical and a critical thinker. She soon discerns if things don't stack up and has a good memory and recall. She is usually efficient, articulate, and thrives on information, making her a good conversationalist, albeit one who soon tires of small talk.

Your Queen of Swords friend has an innate sense of justice and is solution-oriented. If you share your problem, her natural instinct is to logically conclude how it can be solved and what you need to do to overcome it. You might be disappointed if you were just looking for tea and sympathy. She can seem cool and distant at times or almost detached, but she is careful where she places her trust and tends to have a small circle of close and trusted friends.

They make loyal friends and partners who will defend you to the end if they believe you are in the right. The Queen of Swords won't go looking for trouble, but you may be surprised at her strength of character and steely inner determination if you bring it to her door; she is not someone to cross swords with. Being rather dutiful, she may need to be reminded to lighten up and have fun at times.

For email readings, the Queen of Swords can be used to represent a woman with an astrological air sign: Gemini, Libra, or Aquarius.

In career matters, they do well in any areas where they can use their astute mind to its best ability for problem-solving or in fields involving truth and justice, such as: analysis, research, all types of investigative work, logistics, science, IT, legal or law enforcement, military, adjudication, human rights, senior managers/executives.

In readings and in connection with similar cards, they can often represent a female lawyer, due to the various circumstances that involve legal dealings, (divorce, inheritance, property transactions, litigation, etc.,) as shown in the following. In particular, watch for this card connected or surrounded with Justice and the Ace of Pentacles, which can represent legal and official documents, contracts, agreements, etc.

Reversed or Badly Aspected

Being mentally two steps ahead can make them impatient and intolerant with others. They can be sharp-tongued if crossed and emotionally distant if you offend them.

Associations

Supporting or opposing cards don't apply to Kings and Queens as they're neutral and represent people of four distinct personality types.

Queen of Swords Featured Combinations

A King or Queen may represent the client or someone who will be important to their situation. The character description can help identify this person or who will be involved if they're as yet unknown. As before, the card that follows shows what they will bring into being. Look to the surrounding cards to see the extent of the effect they will have and whether it is positive or negative.

> **Ace of Pentacles > Queen of Swords > Knight of Wands:** Financial documents and female legal representative involved in relation to a house move (which proceeds, as the Knight of Wands is the final card).
>
> **Three of Pentacles > Queen of Swords > the Chariot:** A straightforwards lady with strength of character will become involved in a work matter. She helps bring about a successful result for you. (Could be employment law with the right indications and position in the spread or in context to a question).
>
> **Ten of Pentacles > Queen of Swords:** A female lawyer in connection to a family or property matter.
>
> **Justice > Queen of Swords > the Hermit:** Contemplating legal advice received from a female law representative, lawyer, etc.
>
> **The Lovers > Ten of Swords > Queen of Swords > Justice:** Can suggest consulting a female solicitor in relation to divorce proceedings (can also be relevant with the Two or Ten of Cups instead of the Lovers).
>
> **The Emperor > The Hierophant > Justice > Queen of Swords:** Usually official court matters, as it shows higher authorities, such as a judge, female barrister, or client's legal adviser.

KING OF SWORDS

Swords Suit: Intellect, analytical thought, and challenges.

Suit Element: Air. Active. Male energy.

Flow: Brisk

Polarity: Neutral

Multiple Kings: A group of men, men's society. A number of men involved in the situation.

Keywords and Phrases: Enigmatic man. Strong, silent type with backbone.

Applied Meaning

This personality type is enigmatic and can be quite hard to fathom; even those close to them may find it difficult to pinpoint or describe them, which is itself often enough to reveal that you are dealing with a King of Swords. Not usually one for small talk, he may seem a man of few words until he has something meaningful to say, whereupon he may surprise you as he articulates his view-point, in a manner that is precise, well-considered, and that cuts to the chase. He appears to have the ability to flick a switch when solving problems, sifting through facts and parking emotions to one side as he weighs all the information. His conclusion may not be sugar-coated, but he will usually be right.

Swords have strength of character, so the King of Swords has backbone and is usually an unpretentious type who is no-nonsense and straight to the point but steely when challenged. They are strong and protective partners to their friends and loved ones, being firm but fair with a wry wit. They may not wear their heart on their sleeve but still waters run deep; they are fiercely loyal.

For email readings, the King of Swords can be used to represent a man with an astrologcal air sign: Gemini, Libra, or Aquarius.

In career matters, they do well in any areas where they can use their astute mind to its best ability and for problem-solving or fields involving truth and justice, such as: analysis, research, all types of investigative work, logistics, science, IT, legal or law enforcement, military, adjudication, human rights, senior managers/executives.

In readings and in combination with the right cards, they can often represent a man in uniform or a male lawyer, as legal dealings often appear in readings, such as: divorce, inheritance, property transactions, litigation, etc. In particular, watch for this card connected or surrounded with Justice and the Ace of Pentacles, which can represent legal and official documents, contracts, agreements, etc.

Reversed or Badly Aspected

He can be cutting, cold, emotionally detached, impatient, unyielding, domineering—this is not someone to cross swords with!

Associations

Supporting or opposing cards don't apply to Kings and Queens as they're neutral and represent people of four distinct personality types.

King of Swords Featured Combinations

A King or Queen may represent the client or someone who will be important to their situation: check to see what they bring into being by examining the card following them. In future positions it's possible they are as yet unknown to the client, but your description will be helpful in recognising them once encountered.

Seven of Wands > King of Swords > Six of Wands: A strong and straightforwards man lends his support and is in your corner in a situation you feel the need to defend; he will help bring about a successful outcome.

The Hierophant > King of Swords: Can indicate a male official connected to the government.

Death > Ten of Pentacles > King of Swords: Male lawyer in connection with family inheritance and estate matters.

Five of Swords > Five of Pentacles > the Devil > King of Swords: May be financial theft or embezzlement with a cover-up (the King of Swords could represent the police or a lawyer). Note the difference with positioning; if the King of Swords came at the beginning, for example...

King of Swords > Five of Swords > Five of Pentacles > the Devil: ...then a man of this personality description is the source of the problem, as it originates with him and he brings it into being, implying fraud and corruption.

ACE OF PENTACLES

Pentacles Suit: Material affairs. Stability. Grounding and practical.

Suit Element: Earth. Female. Passive.

Flow: Slow but steady

Polarity: Positive

Multiple Aces: Lots of new beginnings across the board.

Keywords and Phrases: New beginning for prosperity. Financial documents. Gifts of gold.

Applied Meaning

The Ace of Pentacles brings a new beginning for wealth and prosperity, suggesting the potential to lay a good and firm foundation upon which to diligently build future success for material affairs. In a wider sense, the material side not only involves finances but that which we need to make our lives more solid, secure, and stable. As the suit of earth, this Ace provides the fertile soil in which you plant your seeds and cultivate your future endeavours.

Pentacles represent material matters, and this card often appears for important paperwork and documentation that in some way holds a financial connection and/or that has a contractual nature, both of which are appropriate at the start of a transaction or agreement. With the relevant cards, it may represent a contract of work in either business or employment; property paperwork such as deeds, contracts, or agreements; an educational award that could affect future earning potential, and even a marriage certificate—when people marry, they are figuratively tying their future fortunes together.

Traditionally, this was a card that could indicate "gifts of gold," so sometimes it may represent jewellery or a ring. Whilst Pentacles may not be the suit we would naturally connect with romantic matters, when this card appears around new relationship cards in a reading it brings a good grounding influence: there's nothing flighty here and represents building something solid and secure for the longer term.

Reversed or Badly Aspected

Misuse of funds or wasting money, financial instability, money doesn't buy happiness.

Associations

    Similar and Supporting Cards: All **Aces** for new beginnings, and **the Fool**. **Justice** (contracts), **Six of Pentacles** (gifts).

    Opposing and Contradictory Cards: Death and **Ten of Swords** (endings), **Five of Pentacles** (material loss).

Ace of Pentacles Featured Combinations

    Ace of Wands > Ace of Pentacles: A new endeavour that holds good promise to do well financially in the future. New work and contract of employment (can also be shown with the **Eight of Pentacles** as new work instead of the Ace of Wands).

Three of Wands > Ace of Pentacles: Initial progress and growth proceeding into a new area that holds good potential. Trade and commercial paperwork; expansion into a potentially lucrative new market.

Knight of Cups > Ace of Pentacles > Two of Cups: Marriage proposal and engagement ring. Can also show Ten of Cups instead of the Two. Similarly, can appear as: **the Lovers > Knight of Cups > Ace of Pentacles**.

Ace of Pentacles > Five of Swords: Possibly counterfeit documents or underhanded financial dealings; leave alone whatever is being peddled, things are too good to be true and not in your best interest, a sentiment strengthened if **the Devil** follows, reinforcing an element of corruption. Also watch for the **Five of Pentacles**, a sure sign you would also lose money.

Six of Swords > Ace of Pentacles: Travel or shipping documents.

Six of Pentacles > Ace of Pentacles: Gifts of gold hold true with this combination and could be in the form of money or jewellery with the potential to be quite generous.

Ace of Pentacles > Seven of Pentacles: Starting a savings or investments plan.

Ace of Pentacles > Ten of Pentacles > Knight of Wands: Property paperwork and contracts for purchase and home move, other indications may also include Justice (legal), the King or Queen of Swords (lawyers), and the King or Queen of Pentacles (financial adviser or money manager).

Ten of Pentacles > Ace of Pentacles: Important financial documents connected to home or family, e.g., insurance policies, trusts, and so on.

The Hierophant > Ten of Cups > Ace of Pentacles: Marriage and official documents, marriage certificate (can also show Justice instead of Ace for the certificate), also the start of married life. Marriage or serious commitment can also appear as: **The Lovers > Ace of Pentacles > Ten of Cups**.

Wheel of Fortune > Ace of Pentacles: A lucky break opens up a new opportunity to do well financially. Whereas, in the opposite order…

Ace of Pentacles > Wheel of Fortune: … may show a lucky ticket!

  * *Collectively, in larger spreads watch for: Ace, Six, Seven, Nine, and Ten of Pentacles appearing anywhere in the spread to indicate an increase and overall financial improvement. The more that are present, the more pronounced the message.*

TWO OF PENTACLES

Pentacles Suit: Material affairs. Stability. Grounding and practical.

Suit Element: Earth. Female. Passive.

Flow: Steady, continuous movement

Polarity: Positive

Multiple Twos: Continuation, development, partnership, balance.

Keywords and Phrases: Maintaining balance. Juggling finances. Multiples.

Applied Meaning

As the image suggests, the Two of Pentacles represents something of a juggling act, whether with finances or other aspects of your life. It can feel as though you're spinning plates at times, but it does suggest that you can successfully maintain the balance needed in a situation.

With finances, the card can indicate careful money management will be needed, whilst at work it may suggest multitasking, wearing more than one hat, or a secondary job or source of income. This card often shows multiples coming into the equation (typically more than one thing simultaneously in play), an aspect I have found to be most reliable in this regard. Some examples are given in the following section.

In general terms, the card can reflect the need to keep something flowing in order to attain a certain equilibrium such as the life-work balance, juggling people, or trying to maintain a status quo between people at work or in the family. As usual, guidance would tend to be influenced by surrounding cards, positioning in the spread, or the question asked.

In combinations, look to the surrounding cards to see what is being balanced or multiplied. If followed by a negative card, such as the Ten of Swords, Death, the Five of Cups, etc., balance will be lost and effort made to no avail.

Reversed or Badly Aspected

Fluctuating fortunes, finances out of balance, making mistakes (dropping the ball).

Associations

> **Similar and Supporting Cards: Justice** (balanced mind), **Temperance** (balanced emotions), **the Magician** (dexterity and skill), **Seven of Cups** (can also show multiples).
>
> **Opposing and Contradictory Cards: Two of Swords, the Hanged Man** (lack of flow, deadlock), **Eight of Swords** (restriction).

Two of Pentacles Featured Combinations

> **Two of Wands > Five of Wands > Two of Pentacles:** You may be trying to keep the peace with warring factions of multiple working partners; at times, it may feel like herding cats, but you can pull it off.

Three of Wands > Ace of Wands > Two of Pentacles: Business expansion and diversifying, adding another string to your bow. Whereas...

Three of Wands > Two of Pentacles: ... may suggest more than one business or careful management of cash flow, particularly if looking to progress or expand. This can hold true in non-commercial settings too; careful manoeuvres to steady the ship.

Two of Pentacles > Ten of Wands: This could be more of a frantic juggling act, taking on too much and becoming overloaded.

Knight of Cups > Two of Pentacles: Suggests multiple offers or invitations.

Two of Pentacles > Three of Swords: Arguments over money management. Multiple quarrels.

Three of Pentacles > Two of Pentacles: More than one type of work or employment, wearing more than one hat, multi-tasking in your main work, can sometimes indicate job sharing.

Five of Pentacles > Two of Pentacles: Careful manoeuvres with a difficult financial situation to keep everything flowing; managing to maintain a balance.

Ten of Pentacles > Two of Pentacles: Usually indicates more than one property. This often appears in situations where members of a family are dealing with a property inheritance as part of the estate (Justice may be present in this type of situation too, but not always).

The Empress > Two of Pentacles: Multiple births or pregnancy. I have also seen...

The Hierophant > the Empress > Two of Pentacles: ... in which IVF treatment at the hospital resulted in two successful embryos.

THREE OF PENTACLES

Pentacles Suit: Material affairs. Stability. Grounding and practical.

Suit Element: Earth. Female. Passive.

Flow: Steady

Polarity: Positive

Multiple Threes: Progress and expansion.

Keywords and Phrases: Skilled work and talents. Main career.

Applied Meaning

The progress and growth in the Three of Pentacles indicates accomplished work, so it can be taken as the main indicator card to represent your primary work or career, or that which you're known for and where your talents and ability naturally shine. It signifies the mastery of your craft in a particular field, gained through diligent effort towards proficiency.

In cards relating to new work, we would usually look for the Eight of Pentacles or Ace of Wands, whereas the Three tends to show work where you are recognised as already being skilled. If connected to new work, it may be a return to a familiar field you have been renowned for, or a talent you already possess and are acclaimed for.

In matters of the heart, it tends to show a connection between work and love; many people meet someone special through their workplace. If the Three of Pentacles appears in the home or love area of the spread, then it may indicate that work is in some way significant or intervening and impacting this area of life. For instance, if a client asked a relationship question concerning a named person and the Three of Pentacles was present in the eighth position of the Celtic Cross (the named person's thoughts on the matter), it would suggest they are currently preoccupied with their work rather than working on the relationship.

Reversed or Badly Aspected

Dissatisfaction in your work, unemployment or loss of work, feeling unappreciated for your efforts, shoddy workmanship.

Associations

Similar and Supporting Cards: The Magician (mastery and skill), **Six of Wands** (acclaimed efforts).

Opposing and Contradictory Cards: Eight of Pentacles (apprenticeship), **Ace of Wands** (new work).

Three of Pentacles Featured Combinations

Ace of Wands > Three of Pentacles: New work or job in an area in which you already have experience or are renowned for (can work in the opposite order too).

Three of Pentacles > Two of Wands: Contributing your work experience to a joint venture or collaboration.

Three of Pentacles > Nine of Wands: Persevering with work though you may feel it's wearing you down (look for a positive card following to see if perseverance will pay off).

Three of Pentacles > Knight of Wands: Work relocation through your job.

Three of Pentacles > Ace of Cups: If single, it can represent a new love relationship in some way connected to your main place of work (can be indirectly). If attached, your main work provides an opportunity for a happy new beginning into your home.

Three of Pentacles > Four of Cups > Eight of Cups: Dissatisfaction in your work causes you to walk away and turn your attention to different avenues.

Three of Pentacles > Ten of Swords: Job loss (if employed), losing important work you may have built up over time (business or self-employed). Watch for …

Three of Pentacles > the Tower > Ten of Swords: … which can point to unexpected redundancy, a layoff, or a sudden end to work that would come as a shock.

Three of Pentacles > Five of Pentacles: Loss of work that affects your income, or an expensive error at work; costly work expenses.

Ten of Pentacles > Three of Pentacles: Can indicate working in a family business, working from home, or a property-related career.

Three of Pentacles > the Fool: Applying and adapting what you know in completely new and innovative ways, transferable skills into new and unfamiliar territory.

Three of Pentacles > the Devil: Can indicate being a workaholic, obsessing over work to the point that it becomes unhealthy.

Four of Pentacles

Pentacles Suit: Material affairs. Stability. Grounding and practical.

Suit Element: Earth. Female. Passive.

Flow: Slow

Polarity: Neutral

Multiple Fours: Structure and stability.

Keywords and Phrases: Material goals. Overcaution. Frugality. Saving money. Banks.

Applied Meaning

The Four of Pentacles is sometimes called the card of the miser; although it can sometimes show that quality, it is usually a broader interpretation—for example, times when you're being frugal and trying to hold on to money for legitimate or sensible reasons. For instance, someone might be seriously saving for a particular financial goal such as a deposit on a house, squirreling away funds to improve stability, or, if money has been in short supply, trying to make it go further to make funds last.

In relationships and in more general terms, this card can represent someone being overly cautious or hesitant, perhaps with regards to getting involved or moving forwards, especially if they have experienced hurt or trauma in the past. Surrounding cards should help point you in the right direction.

No matter the circumstances, the Four of Pentacles can act as a reminder that you may need to loosen your grip slightly and take a calculated risk while following due diligence. In work matters, it can suggest being focussed and prepared to work hard towards a material goal.

In practical terms, it can show savings accounts but also banks or money-lenders due to the prudent approach and often stringent measures needed in an application process. This is an excellent card for organising budgets or arranging savings.

Reversed or Badly Aspected

The structure of the material side of life can become more rigid and extreme, such as: avarice and greed, hoarding, excessive fear of loss, lack mentality, with-holding.

Associations

Similar and Supportive Cards: Four of Swords (consolidation), **Seven of Pentacles** (investment), **the Hermit** (prudence).

Opposing and Contradictory Cards: Five of Pentacles (loss), **Six of Pentacles** (sharing), **the Fool** (carefree), **Temperance** (moderation).

Four of Pentacles Featured Combinations

Ace of Wands > Four of Pentacles: Where the pedal meets the metal, a new project will require structured and concerted effort; just ensure that your stamina matches your enthusiasm to see it through, as caution could creep in.

Seven of Cups > Four of Pentacles > Two of Pentacles: Hedging your bets whilst doubling down on your efforts.

Four of Pentacles > Two of Pentacles: Being careful with finances to keep the flow going, balancing the books and keeping a check on finances.

Six of Pentacles > Four of Pentacles: Banking or holding on to a cash payment or gift. May not feel inclined to share the generosity shown to you; other indications may suggest this is the right approach for the circumstances.

Four of Pentacles > Seven of Pentacles: Saving for a rainy day, setting up a long-term investment plan that should pay off.

The Hierophant > Four of Pentacles: Usually a bank or financial institution (normally lenders).

The Lovers > Four of Pentacles: Holding back emotionally, possibly cautious of becoming involved in a relationship and getting cold feet.

Four of Pentacles > Strength: You're prepared to work hard towards material goals and will endure whatever is necessary to achieve them; courage and quiet determination will see you through.

Four of Pentacles > the Hermit: A double dose of caution with this combination can reveal hesitancy to move forwards. In money matters, it can represent long-term saving plans that are risk-averse: safe, not high-risk, such as with banks or building societies, not stocks and/or shares or similar.

Wheel of Fortune > Four of Pentacles: A risk you don't feel prepared to take; not taking any chances, feeling risk-averse. An overly cautious approach could prevent optimising opportunities.

Four of Pentacles > the Devil: An unhealthy financial habit; hoarding.

FIVE OF PENTACLES

Pentacles Suit: Material affairs. Stability. Grounding and practical.

Suit Element: Earth. Female. Passive.

Flow: Unstable; barren land

Polarity: Negative

Multiple Fives: Challenges and instability.

Keywords and Phrases: Temporary hardship. Financial problem or loss. Shortage of funds.

Applied Meaning

As a card of lack, the Five of Pentacles brings the progression of the figure's fears from the Four into being. The unstable nature of Fives, the halfway tipping point in the suit of material affairs, indicates financial instability, although often of a temporary nature.

The Five of Pentacles is the main card to look for in relation to financial losses of all kinds; it can be a straightforwards lack of funds, or indirectly in the form of an unavoidable yet unanticipated expense that suddenly blows a hole in your pocket and upsets the bank balance. Either way, it suggests that money will be lacking or in short supply and could create some inconvenience.

The root or preceding card will show where the problem stems from and in future positions can help provide warning of a lean period ahead, with the suggestion to prepare and take whatever action is possible to avert or minimise losses. The stained-glass window in the background suggests being careful not to miss any valid opportunity for help and support that may be available to you.

As with other cards that have negative connotations, we tend to anticipate the worst, but it's important to keep things in perspective: usually this card reflects a shortage of funds or receiving less than was expected, catching you unawares.

On a more personal level, sometimes the Five of Pentacles can suggest a sense of desolation, or when all hope feels lost at the bottom of a downward spiral. You may feel others have not been supportive, although the emotional aspect is one I tend to associate more with the Five of Cups.

Reversed or Badly Aspected

Recovering from a difficult financial problem, emerging from a material crisis, regaining position, a narrow escape and danger averted.

Associations

Similar and Supporting Cards: Five of Cups (sense of loss), **Four of Cups** (care not to miss a valid opportunity).

Opposing and Contradictory Cards: Six of Pentacles (generosity and gifts), **Seven of Pentacles** (payments and rewards), **Nine of Pentacles** (financial comfort), **Ten of Pentacles** (material stability), **the Empress** (abundant harvest), **the Star** (hope), **the Sun** (abundant blessings).

Five of Pentacles Featured Combinations

Three of Wands > Five of Pentacles: May have to rein in spending temporarily; future plans are too expensive in their current form. In commercial business, overtrading or overexpansion will create a financial problem; plans may be overambitious and overreaching. A material snarl-up in the pipeline.

Knight of Wands > Five of Pentacles: House move expenses: make provision as could be more expensive than budgeted for, with hidden costs.

Knight of Cups > Ten of Pentacles > Five of Pentacles: A property offer is lower than your expectations.

Five of Pentacles > Two of Swords: Financial loss creates a deadlock that prevents forwards movement. Be careful not to ignore a financial problem as inaction won't solve it and creates a holding pattern.

Five of Pentacles > Four of Pentacles: Reining in finances; use budgets and financial planning to accommodate a temporary downturn.

Six of Pentacles > Five of Pentacles: Money coming in going straight back out. If both are in future positions, can show anticipated money fails to arrive.

Eight of Pentacles > Five of Pentacles: Taking a new position but with a drop in salary; downshifting, which may be a necessary move for a longer-term career goal. New work may pay less than you hoped or come with additional personal expenses.

Ten of Pentacles > Five of Pentacles: Can indicate being asset-rich but cash-poor. An unanticipated bill or expense connected to the home.

Ten of Pentacles > Five of Pentacles > Three of Swords: Disagreement over family finances; financial problems could cause upset and upheavals.

The Fool > Five of Pentacles: A financially irresponsible action, possibly through lack of knowledge or experience; check all the details before jumping into a new opportunity—it doesn't appear financially viable.

Five of Pentacles > The Magician: By taking a proactive approach to tackle a financial problem you can find an innovative solution.

Five of Pentacles > The Devil: Overspending will come back to bite you and bog you down. Can be a shopaholic tendency.

Six of Pentacles

Pentacles Suit: Material affairs. Stability. Grounding and practical.

Suit Element: Earth. Female. Passive.

Flow: Steady

Polarity: Positive

Multiple Sixes: Harmony and improvement.

Keywords and Phrases: Generosity, gifts and sharing. Charity.

Applied Meaning

Following nicely after the Five, the Six of Pentacles brings just what you need when in such circumstances; it indicates generosity, gifts, and sharing. It can point to a charitable or generous benefactor, someone acting kindly and feeling well-disposed towards you, or even dispensing favours in your direction that aren't necessarily money but usually something of material worth.

The wealthy merchant in the card appears to reflect the charitable act; the six Pentacles that surround him and his balanced scales may suggest he holds enough for his own benefit and has enough to share with others. As one of the five cards that can collectively represent financial increase, it tends to suggest an improvement in finances or material circumstances through money given (see the following section). In whatever form, it suggests something of material worth coming to you whether as a gift, payment, salary increase or bonus, or even money being shared out.

In relationships, it can reflect a giving nature and spirit of generosity, the aspect of sharing and harmonious flow of giving and receiving. This card usually indicates receiving a gift but perhaps one that in turn provides the opportunity for the recipient to also share their good fortune with others. A strange quirk of this card is that, in combination with certain others, it represented the stock market and has since proven reliable in this regard.

Reversed or Badly Aspected

Selfishness, reluctance or refusal to help others, favours with strings attached, not meeting financial obligations.

Associations

> **Similar and Supporting Cards: Ace of Pentacles** (gifts of gold). Financial improvement aspect: **Seven, Nine,** and **Ten of Pentacles**.
>
> **Opposing and Contradictory Cards: Four of Pentacles** (withholding), **Five of Pentacles** (financial loss).

Six of Pentacles Featured Combinations

Ace of Wands > Six of Pentacles: New work that brings some financial increase, charitable project, favours and help from others in your new venture.

Three of Wands > Six of Pentacles > Ace of Pentacles: Trading in stocks and shares; stock market (longer-term investment). Also ...

Three of Wands > Six of Pentacles > Two of Pentacles: ... trading in commodities (in-and-out, shorter-term trading).

*The Hierophant may sometimes also feature as a traditional institution but only if preceding the Three of Wands, which indicates the commercial aspect.

Six of Wands > Six of Pentacles: Promotion and pay increase, recognition through work with financial bonus.

Knight of Wands > Six of Pentacles: House move and housewarming gifts.

Three of Cups > Six of Pentacles: Celebration gifts (surrounding cards should advise what type of celebration).

Five of Pentacles > Six of Pentacles: Charity; generous help and support coming to your aid in a financial matter.

The Hierophant > Six of Pentacles: A charitable foundation and institution. Could also be charity shown towards you from such an institution. In a work situation, it can indicate favourable treatment (possible bonus payment) from a large organisation.

The Lovers > Six of Pentacles: Gifts from a romantic partner; giving and receiving in the relationship.

Temperance > Six of Pentacles: May be a peace offering.

Six of Pentacles > The Devil: A gift with strings attached, possibly a bribe.

Death > Ten of Pentacles > Six of Pentacles: Can indicate a family legacy, inheritance.

SEVEN OF PENTACLES

Pentacles Suit: Material affairs. Stability. Grounding and practical.

Suit Element: Earth. Female. Passive.

Flow: Steady and consistent

Polarity: Positive

Multiple Sevens: A cycle change.

Keywords and Phrases: Reward for efforts, payments. Investments. Gathering your harvest but still work in progress.

Applied Meaning

The farmer and his crop reference the methodical cycle, reflective of the steady and consistent effort required over the seasons, indicating toiling with ongoing and steady progress. Preparations are now being contemplated for when the harvest can finally be gathered and the value realised before the whole process begins again.

The Seven of Pentacles brings the results of your patience, preparation, and hard work. It is the moment you begin to reap the rewards of your labours—something you have been diligently beavering towards now starts to pay some dividends. Where the Six indicates gifts given, the Seven brings payments for efforts expended (normally something dilligently worked for), whether through work or saving investments. As such, this card usually represents payments, with an increase in finances and improvement to circumstances.

Whilst this is a card of fruitfulness and fulfilment, it isn't usually an end unto itself but more of a work in progress, suggesting an ongoing process through "cultivating" one's "crop." In work situations, it would be similar to the ongoing exchange of time for money, continuous employment, payment for completed work, royalties, or incremental payments. It can also represent payouts from investments or stock dividends, i.e., nurturing your nest egg.

In broader terms, "gathering in your harvest" can be taken more metaphorically, although there is usually a financial connection in there somewhere. Just as with the cycle of a harvest, this is a slow-moving card that will not be hurried, although beneficial aspects are beginning to show.

Reversed or Badly Aspected

Disappointing yields, expenditure exceeds income, behaving imprudently.

Associations

Similar and Supporting Cards: The Empress (fruitful harvest), **Knight of Pentacles** (longstanding results forthcoming), to some extent the **Four of Pentacles** (hard work, savings), **Temperance** (patience).

Opposing and Contradictory Cards: Four of Cups (apathy), **Four of Swords** (inactivity), **Five of Pentacles** (financial lack).

Seven of Pentacles Featured Combinations

Two of Wands > Seven of Pentacles: A working partnership proves to be productive and will bring reward for efforts, which should lead to financial improvement.

Eight of Wands > Seven of Pentacles: Usually a payment through the post or electronic bank transfer, money coming in quickly.

Four of Swords > Seven of Pentacles: Consolidating your position and resources will reap the benefits but it will be an ongoing process for some time.

Page of Swords > Seven of Pentacles: There may be a slight delay, but the payment will come through.

Two of Pentacles > Seven of Pentacles: Can indicate multiple streams of income or recurring payments.

Three of Pentacles > Seven of Pentacles: A work project coming to fruition; receiving payment; the ongoing cycle of work and wages, continuous employment.

Four of Pentacles > Seven of Pentacles: Savings and investment plan for the longer term, patience required but should yield favourable results; interest and dividend payments from investments. Working hard brings rewards.

Seven of Pentacles > Five of Pentacles: Expenditure exceeds income; there may be more going out than coming in or not sufficient to meet an expense. Short-changed.

Seven of Pentacles > Nine of Pentacles: Would tend to indicate a fairly substantial sum of money coming in.

The Fool > Seven of Pentacles: An unexpected payment that comes as a nice surprise.

Seven of Pentacles > the Empress: The fruitful and abundant harvest! Rewards may be greater than initially anticipated (overlap and reinforced meaning strengthens interpretation).

The Devil > Seven of Pentacles > the Moon: Questionable and hidden financial activity; may suggest dodgy dealings, possible money laundering, or criminal activity and cover-up. (The **Five of Swords** in place of the Moon would be similar).

EIGHT OF PENTACLES

Pentacles Suit: Material affairs. Stability. Grounding and practical.

Suit Element: Earth. Female. Passive.

Flow: Steady

Polarity: Positive

Multiple Eights: Flow and movement.

Keywords and Phrases: New work or study.

Applied Meaning

The Eight of Pentacles is often referred to as the apprenticeship card, so it usually signifies new work or employment; even if you start a new post in a familiar field, it can still take time to get your footing and the lay of the land when joining a new company, and there's often a probationary period. For those in business or self-employed, it tends to bring in new work or clients.

Training or study courses of all descriptions can feature both in formal or informal settings, indicating that you're broadening your talents and developing your skill set as you polish and hone the skills of your craft. Diligent and industrious, the card shows you keeping your head down and focussing upon the task at hand. For some it can indicate working on a hobby or talent and developing it further into a money-making venture.

In divination, this is one of the main indicator cards I would use to represent new work, a meaning that—unlike some cards whose meanings can change depending on the topic—does not deviate. The theme of new work remains, no matter the circumstance. For instance, in love situations this card still shows that a new job is relevant in some way—if someone wants to know why they haven't heard from their partner, this card may indicate that the partner is engrossed in new work. Or if looking for love, it may show that their attention will be fully absorbed in a new work matter which may need to take precedence, or perhaps meeting someone through a new job. In relation to matters concerning the home, it may show the effect of a new job on the home and family.

Reversed or Badly Aspected

Lack of work, unemployment, sloppy efforts, disillusionment, boredom with a repetitive environment or lower skill set that doesn't utilise your talents; a lack of ambition.

Associations

> **Similar and Supporting Cards: Ace of Wands** (new venture), **Seven of Pentacles** (diligent effort), and to some degree the **Four of Pentacles** (in terms of working hard).

> **Opposing and Contradictory Cards: The Magician** and **Three of Pentacles** (skill and mastery).

Eight of Pentacles Featured Combinations

Eight of Pentacles > Four of Wands: New work finds structure and settles down nicely.

Six of Wands > the Emperor > Eight of Pentacles: Being promoted into a new job with a senior role. If the Eight of Pentacles came at the beginning, it would show making swift advancement in a new job towards a senior position in a fairly short period of time.

Nine of Wands > Eight of Pentacles > Three of Cups: Perseverance pays off as new work arrives and brings cause for celebration. Can also apply if you've been trying to get into a study programme.

Eight of Pentacles > Eight of Cups: Abandoning a course before completion, or not staying in new employment due to dissatisfaction.

Knight of Cups > Eight of Pentacles: An offer of new work or study placement.

Eight of Pentacles > Two of Pentacles: Taking a second job, job sharing, or new work that involves combining two separate roles.

Eight of Pentacles > Three of Pentacles: Making good progression from apprentice to mastery in your field. Whereas …

Three of Pentacles > Eight of Pentacles: … in this order, new work in a field where you're already experienced or have an easily transferable skill set. For business and those self-employed, can indicate new work or clients. Workplace training course.

Eight of Pentacles > Nine of Pentacles: New work that brings an uplift in finances and material improvement, could be a substantial wage increase.

The Hierophant > Eight of Pentacles > the Hermit: Formal education or study institution, university, etc. (can be in any order).

Eight of Pentacles > the Hanged Man: New work may feel like a dead-end job or not progressing as quickly as you would like—you may reassess your position. In connection to career matters, the Hanged Man can sometimes represent the glass-ceiling effect.

NINE OF PENTACLES

Pentacles Suit: Material affairs. Stability. Grounding and practical.

Suit Element: Earth. Female. Passive.

Flow: A leisurely pace

Polarity: Positive

Multiple Nines: Penultimate moment, almost there, tying up loose ends towards completion.

Keywords and Phrases: Material ease and comfort. Luxury items. Self-reliance.

Applied Meaning

Nine golden Pentacles hang from the abundant and blossoming vine now laden with fruit, adding to the opulence of the verdant scene. The woman gazes at the falcon on her hand with an expression of pride and satisfaction; birds of prey as pets were historically considered status symbols, as only the wealthy could afford to keep them.

The Nine of Pentacles suggests that everything in your garden is flourishing. As the penultimate number of the material suit, we now reach the stage where you can find enjoyment in the fruits of your labours achieved through prudent and diligent efforts; it is a time of ease, a comfortable lifestyle. It can suggest a substantial sum of money or at least more than you usually deal with on a daily basis, enough to provide material ease and the enjoyment of some home comforts. As a card of plenty, it can also represent luxury items, something a little bit fancy and special.

This card usually appears for those who are self-reliant, financially independent, secure, and self-sufficient through their own efforts or in their own right, regardless of whether they are single or attached. As such, it can represent money from your own efforts, although surrounding cards may show it in other ways, such as receiving a substantial sum, enjoying material pleasures, etc.

As always, the accompanying cards will determine the circumstances, but it brings material ease and an improvement to finances. Whatever you may have been cultivating (shown by the preceding card) results in prompt accomplishment and successful fulfilment.

Reversed or Badly Aspected

Unrestrained indulgence or overspending, squandering resources, diminishing returns, financial embarrassment, an ill-conceived and failing vanity project. Codependency issues.

Associations

Similar and Supporting Cards: The Empress (abundant harvest), Ten of Pentacles (wealth and stability).

Opposing and Contradictory Cards: Five of Pentacles (financial lack).

Nine of Pentacles Featured Combinations

Three of Wands > Nine of Pentacles: Trading in luxury goods, but can also suggest future plans hold successful financial gains.

Nine of Pentacles > Four of Wands: A significant financial improvement leads to greater stability.

Two of Cups > Nine of Pentacles: Standing in your own identity within a relationship; self-reliance and personal empowerment.

Two of Cups > Four of Wands > Nine of Pentacles: A luxurious short break with your partner.

Three of Cups > Nine of Pentacles: A black-tie event or fancy occasion, something a little bit special (posh frocks and champagne)!

Nine of Pentacles > Six of Swords: A substantial sum brings financial improvement and greater material security for the future; past difficulties left behind. Possibly a luxury trip or cruise, but most particularly when other travel cards present.

Two of Pentacles > Nine of Pentacles: Financially pulling the rabbit out the hat; the Midas touch after lots of juggling, money may come from more than one source (this Two suggests multiples).

Three of Pentacles > Nine of Pentacles: Prosperous work and financial improvement from endeavours.

Five of Pentacles > Nine of Pentacles: Rags to riches; the famine and the feast, a fairly swift turnaround to financial fortunes.

Six of Pentacles > Nine of Pentacles: Receiving a luxury gift, or a generous sum.

Wheel of Fortune > Nine of Pentacles: Could be a lucky gamble that pays off, a favourable change of fortunes in your finances.

Judgement > Ace of Wands > Nine of Pentacles: A new project that has roots in the past being revived and paying off handsomely.

TEN OF PENTACLES

Pentacles Suit: Material affairs. Stability. Grounding and practical.

Suit Element: Earth. Female. Passive.

Flow: Steady

Polarity: Positive

Multiple Tens: A period of completion.

Keywords and Phrases: Home and family. Material security. Property. Wealth and prosperity.

Applied Meaning

Our journey through the Pentacles suit shows a neat progression as we navigate the material plane of life, arriving at the destination and completion in the Ten. As the final number of the suit, it represents the ultimate for wealth and prosperity with the comfort and security that this brings.

The Ten of Pentacles indicates the material stability of home and family. It covers the place you call home and includes your family clan and relatives. Not only does it refer to whomever you live with, it also includes the deep roots and foundations of intergenerational links in your family tree. In the right combination, it can show a family inheritance.

Property matters often feature, which can include secondary and inherited property, but most particularly in relation to the family home itself, which is usually the biggest investment or expenditure for most people. The Ten of Cups is the beating heart of the home, whereas the Ten of Pentacles tends to represent the more practical aspects for a settled family life and the stability of the family abode, together with the enjoyment of those things. In ideal situations, you find the two together (see Nine of Cups combinations as an example); love may be a "many-splendored thing," but money pays the bills and keeps the wolf from the door!

Reversed or Badly Aspected

Problems within the family, instability and insecurity regarding material matters, property or inheritance disputes, material losses that impact the home.

Associations

> **Similar and Supporting Cards: The Hierophant** (tradition of family institution), **the Emperor** and **Four of Wands** (stability), **Nine of Pentacles** (material comfort), **Ten of Cups**, although more connected to an emotionally settled family life.

> **Opposing and Contradictory Cards: Five of Pentacles** (financial instability), **Three of Swords** (family upheavals).

Ten of Pentacles Featured Combinations

Knight of Wands > Ten of Pentacles: The overlap reinforces a home move and property matters.

Two of Cups > Ten of Pentacles: Relationship stability and developing to the next stage, becoming more settled and setting up home together.

Ten of Pentacles > Three of Cups: Family get-together, gathering of your clan for a special occasion.

Ten of Pentacles > Knight of Cups: Property offer being received, or can be an invitation from family.

Ten of Pentacles > Three of Swords: Family needling and squabbles can raise stormy emotions, could be a property matter that leads to a dispute; upset and upheaval.

Ten of Pentacles > Two of Pentacles: Second home, or multiple properties; juggling family finances.

Ten of Pentacles > Three of Pentacles: Working from home, family or home business. Sometimes a property business (depending upon question or position in the spread), although the Three of Wands would usually represent the commercial aspect.

Ten of Pentacles > Five of Pentacles: Family finances take a hit, an unexpected bill connected to home or a property.

Ten of Pentacles > Justice: Would usually show legal documents or agreements in connection with home and family or a property matter.

Death > Ten of Pentacles: Family inheritance matters; can also include: **Justice, Six of Pentacles,** and **Ace of Pentacles** (also see the **Death** card).

Ten of Pentacles > Judgement: Home or property makeover and revamping, renovations, restoration, refurbishment, etc.

PAGE OF PENTACLES

Pentacles Suit: Material affairs. Stability. Grounding and practical.

Suit Element: Earth. Passive. Female.

Flow: Slow and steady

Polarity: Positive/Neutral

Multiple Pages: Multiple messages, children's group.

Keywords and Phrases: News concerning money or study. A practical
and placid child.

Applied Meaning

Primarily, the Page of Pentacles brings messages of a material nature, usually news you are pleased to receive, unless it is followed by a card indicating otherwise. There are two sides to the coin, so with the right surrounding cards or in a particular context, it can suggest news of an academic or educational nature, such as a course or study programmes, for instance.

Where appropriate, the secondary meaning provides the personality description to represent a minor. The Page of Pentacles child is steady and reliable, methodical and thorough in their approach to any task they are given or undertake. They can be quite academic or, alternatively, good with practical tasks and things requiring manual dexterity. They follow instructions diligently and to the letter, are usually sensible and well-behaved, and take most things in their stride. The Pentacles child thrives in an environment of order and routine.

Reversed or Badly Aspected

Unfavourable news regarding finance or study. As a child, stubborn, lacking drive and motivation, unimaginative.

Associations

Similar and Supporting Cards: As messages, **Page of Wands**, **Page of Cups**, **Eight of Wands**, **Six of Wands**. **Eight of Pentacles** (study).

Opposing and Contradictory Cards: Page of Swords (delayed news).

Page of Pentacles Featured Combinations

Page of Pentacles > Four of Wands: Good news concerning finances leads to stability and a settled situation.

Page of Pentacles > Five of Wands: There could be misunderstandings or conflicting views concerning finance; this news creates petty obstacles and perhaps a few financial hoops to navigate.

Knight of Cups > Page of Pentacles > Four of Cups: A financial offer or proposal leaves you feeling flat.

Page of Swords > Page of Pentacles: Financial news will be delayed, although it will arrive. Whereas, in the opposite order...

Page of Pentacles > Page of Swords: … financial news could be slightly disappointing and not what you hoped to hear. If the situation in question concerns a Pentacles child, it can show some forthcoming problems in the situation surrounding them, although usually minor.

Page of Pentacles > Five of Pentacles: Bills; could be an expense that leaves you out of pocket to create a temporary hiccup. But if these cards are additionally followed by any of the following, then it would also show:

Page of Pentacles > Five of Pentacles > Ten of Wands: … this puts you under pressure;

Page of Pentacles > Five of Pentacles > Eight of Swords: … leaves you in a fix;

Page of Pentacles > Five of Pentacles > Nine of Swords: … creates anxiety.

Page of Pentacles > Seven of Pentacles: Good news with the arrival of a payment. The **Nine of Pentacles** instead of the Seven would usually suggest a more substantial sum being received.

Page of Pentacles > Eight of Pentacles: The reinforced meaning gives a strong indication of good news for a study placement or training course, particularly for a child. Alternatively, news concerning new work will have a positive impact on your finances.

Judgement > Page of Pentacles > the Empress: Material news that has roots in the past reaches fulfilment.

KNIGHT OF PENTACLES

Pentacles Suit: Material affairs. Stability. Grounding and practical.

Suit Element: Earth. Passive. Female.

Flow: Slowly plodding

Polarity: Positive

Multiple Knights: Lots of action and movement.

Keywords and Phrases: A longstanding situation. Results finally forthcoming.

Applied Meaning

Contrary to his fellow Knights, the steed of the Knight of Pentacles is motionless and heavier set with the appearance of a dray or work horse. In the background we see furrowed fields, suggesting the steady and more practical aspects of the suit.

All the Knights represent an action or event of some description, and the Knight of Pentacles indicates a longstanding situation or something that has gone on for quite some time finally coming to fruition. Positioning can indicate which way to go with this card: at the beginning it can represent a slow burn that eventually catches light, whereas closing the sequence it shows the results will finally arrive.

This is a slow-moving card that suggests steady progress and details taken care of in a methodical fashion, not trying to cut corners along the way. It may be a situation in which you have plodded along over a lengthy period, sometimes even to the extent of having almost given up expecting a result. Whilst usually a positive card, it can sometimes appear in less favourable situations, still indicating a long-standing matter coming to a head, although not of the positive variety.

Reversed or Badly Aspected

Lack of progress, stagnation, inertia.

Associations

Similar and Supporting Cards: All Knights indicate movement, although the Knight of Pentacles reflects a much slower energy and, in this regard, **the Hermit** and **Temperance** (patience); **Strength** (endurance); **Nine of Wands** (perseverance).

Opposing and Contradictory Cards: Eight of Wands and **Knight of Swords** (speed), **the Chariot** (forceful driving energy).

Knight of Pentacles Featured Combinations

Knight of Pentacles > Ace of Wands: Finally starting a project that may have been a long time in the making. In the opposite order …

Ace of Wands > Knight of Pentacles: … a new venture for the long haul, slow and steady; don't expect quick results, take your time.

Knight of Pentacles > Ace of Wands > the Empress > Nine of Cups: A long-awaited and longed-for pregnancy.

Knight of Pentacles > Ace of Cups: A slow-burn relationship that finally ignites; it may have taken a long time to reach this point, so it can suggest someone you've known for some time.

Knight of Pentacles > Three of Swords: A quarrel that has been building over a period of time over a long-standing issue. Similarly...

Knight of Pentacles > Ten of Pentacles > Three of Swords: ...can indicate a long-standing family feud or one that has been simmering and gathering steam, particularly in relation to family inheritances (which is quite common).

Knight of Pentacles > Knight of Swords: This situation takes a long time to find its feet; you may have been methodically working towards a goal over a lengthy period, but once events unfold, they will do so with chaotic speed.

Seven of Pentacles > Knight of Pentacles: A long-standing investment finally comes to fruition (this combination can also work in the opposite order).

Knight of Pentacles > Eight of Pentacles: Finally landing a new job or study placement, perhaps a position you have long sought.

Strength > Knight of Pentacles: Endurance and tenacity will eventually pay off when matters bear fruit, as they will in the fullness of time.

Justice > Nine of Wands > Knight of Pentacles: A prolonged legal matter that has required great perseverance will conclude at last.

The Hanged Man > Knight of Pentacles: Although events will eventually conclude with great relief, this combination suggests it could be a protracted matter.

QUEEN OF PENTACLES

Pentacles Suit: Material affairs. Stability. Grounding and practical.

Suit Element: Earth. Passive. Female.

Flow: Steady

Polarity: Neutral

Multiple Queens: Indicates numerous women involved in the situation. Women's group or society.

Keywords and Phrases: Practical and well-organised woman.

Applied Meaning

The Queen of Pentacles is a capable woman, steady and reliable, excellent with detail and taking care of practicalities. They are great organisers who make "to-do" lists, neatly file everything away, and enjoy the familiarity of routine. They are good at following through from start to finish with an orderly and methodical approach. Solid and dependable, they rarely flap and tend to take most things in stride. They prefer the safety and security of a long-term plan rather than leaving things to chance or an ad hoc basis.

Your Queen of Pentacles friend is highly organised but not terribly keen on spontaneity or surprises; if you're visiting, be sure to let them know in advance so they are prepared for your arrival in her own way, rather than landing on the doorstep unannounced. They can seem the polar opposite to the King and Queen of Wands but they actually work really well together: Wands go out and make things happen to create activity whilst Pentacles organise the chaos behind them, following through and making sure everything happens as it should and within the right time frame. Queen of Pentacles are solid as a rock but can become staid and set in their ways.

In career matters, they excel in any fields where they can use their natural organisation talents and attention to detail that requires a methodical and thorough approach, such as: accounting, administration, auditing, curating, engineering, all financial fields, human resources, library sciences, proofreading and editing, and teaching. On the other side of the Pentacles coin, some are good with their hands and more inclined towards practical skills and/or anything connected to the earth, such as: agriculture, animal services, catering or food, construction trades, land and property, horticulture, mining and precious metals.

If you are relating them to astrological sun signs, Pentacles are aligned with the astrological earth signs: Taurus, Virgo, and Capricorn, which can be useful in email readings where the client isn't present for a two-way conversation. Because sun signs are not always known, character description is usually a better indicator.

In readings, the King and Queen of Pentacles often represent financial advisers, bank managers, or similar, especially when the King or Queen of Swords is also present (lawyers), in relation to property matters, inheritances, or material issues. With house moves and property matters, the following are often present: Ace of Pentacles, Ten of Pentacles, Knight of Wands, King or Queen of Pentacles (money manager), King or Queen of Swords (lawyer).

Reversed or Badly Aspected

Can become fixed to set routines or set in their ways and avoid change; may lack imagination; perfectionism; being overly concerned with the need for a sense of security; materialism.

Associations

Supporting or opposing cards don't apply to Kings and Queens, as they are neutral and represent adults of four distinct personality types.

Queen of Pentacles Featured Combinations

In combinations, a King or Queen may represent the client (if they fit the personality description of the card) or someone who will be instrumental to their situation. You can see if they will have a positive or negative influence by the card that follows them.

> **Three of Wands > Queen of Pentacles > Two of Pentacles:** Commercial or trading enterprise, possibly a business expansion; may be a female accountant or money manager who helps balance the books or cash flow.
>
> **Four of Wands > Queen of Pentacles > Three of Cups:** This woman could be a wedding or event planner, as she sits central to two cards that reinforce one another for wedding proceedings. This combination would also be the same if the Queen came at the beginning of the three cards.
>
> **Queen of Pentacles > Knight of Cups:** Indicates that the offer or invitation originates and comes directly from a mature woman of this description; solid, reliable, and someone who pays attention to detail.
>
> **Three of Pentacles > Queen of Pentacles > Seven of Swords:** This practical and methodical woman is connected to your main work, suggesting a delicate situation around her is being handled with great care; she may assist you in developing a strategy.
>
> **Queen of Pentacles > Four of Pentacles > Ace of Pentacles:** Important financial document from a money manager and financial institution (bank manager—finance organisation—financial document).
>
> **The Lovers > Queen of Pentacles > Ten of Wands:** Pressure on a relationship is coming directly from the influence of a lady of this description.

KING OF PENTACLES

Pentacles Suit: Material affairs. Stability. Grounding and practical.

Suit Element: Earth. Passive. Female energy.

Flow: Steady

Polarity: Neutral

Multiple Kings: A number of different men involved in the situation. A men's group or society.

Keywords and Phrases: Steady and reliable man.

Applied Meaning

The King of Pentacles is stable, calm, and dependable—the epitome of Mr. Reliable, solid as a rock. He takes a practical approach to matters and rarely gets flustered. If you are taking a trip together, he would probably enjoy researching the area in advance and have the itinerary planned down to the last detail, so you wouldn't need to worry about anything—he would have considered every possibility. If anything should go awry, he would calmly measure up the practicalities in an untroubled manner without any drama—he's the man with a plan!

The King of Pentacles personality type is shrewd and astute and has a keen eye for a good deal and a bargain. They consider things carefully and rationally and will not be rushed or bulldozed into a decision or action before feeling ready to do so. They are usually hardworking and tend to quietly plough systematically towards their goals without trying to cut corners, so this can make them successful in their field if they so choose, but security rather than ambition is usually the driving force.

In career matters, they excel in any fields where they can use their natural organisation talents and attention to detail to things that require a methodical and thorough approach, such as: accounting, administration, auditing, curation, engineering, all financial fields, human resources, library sciences, proofreading and editing, and teaching. There are two sides to the Pentacles coin, so some are good with their hands and more inclined towards practical skills and/or anything connected to the earth, such as: agriculture, animal services, catering or food services, construction trades, land and property, horticulture, mining and precious metals.

For email readings, the King of Pentacles can be used to represent a man with an astrological earth sign: Taurus, Virgo, or Capricorn.

In readings, the King and Queen of Pentacles often represent financial advisers, bank managers, or similar; this is particularly so when the King or Queen of Swords is also present (lawyers), in relation to property matters, inheritances, or material issues. With house moves and property matters, the following are often present: Ace of Pentacles, Ten of Pentacles, Knight of Wands, King or Queen of Pentacles (money manager), King or Queen of Swords (lawyer).

Reversed or Badly Aspected
Can be stubborn to the point of exasperation; an immovable object; being set in their ways, lacking imagination, materialism.

Associations
Supporting or opposing cards don't apply to Kings and Queens, as they are neutral and represent people of four distinct personality types.

King of Pentacles Featured Combinations
A King or Queen may represent the client (if they fit the personality description) or someone who will be relevant to their situation. If you have a preceding card, it can show how they came into the picture, what they are connected to, or the initial seed of their involvement. Check the card that follows to see what they are bringing into the situation.

Three of Wands > King of Pentacles > Ten of Swords: Progress and future plans take a backwards step and evaporate in due course, as this man's involvement leads to failure of previous plans. In areas of the spread that represent work or home, it could indicate reliance upon a bank manager, financier, or similar, as the Three suggests plans for expansion.

Nine of Wands > King of Pentacles > Ace of Swords: You may be dealing with a trying situation, but a steady and reliable man helps to bring about a triumphant resolution.

King of Pentacles > Five of Swords > Judgement: This suggests a repeat performance regarding an issue of dishonesty involving a man with the King of Pentacles personality. If it appeared in a different order, such as:

King of Pentacles > Judgement > Five of Swords: ... this ordering would still show something untowards occurring, but Judgement indicates the King is a man the client will reconnect with. Unfortunately, he appears to have ulterior motives—the situation can't be trusted.

III

The Major Arcana
Applied Meanings and Combinations

0—The Fool

Major Arcana (Trumps or Triumphs): Symbolic life experiences. Worldly affairs. The spiritual journey.

Flow: Sudden, unpredictable

Polarity: Positive

Multiple Majors: Milestones and significant life events. Catalyst.

Keywords and Phrases: Surprise or an unexpected situation. New and unfamiliar. Potential.

Applied Meaning

When the Fool appears in your reading, it suggests an unexpected or surprise event that seems to land as if from out of nowhere, completely out of the blue. It holds an unpredictable and spontaneous nature but is usually positive unless followed by less favourable cards.

The moment is ripe with fresh possibilities and unexplored potential that can take you down a new and unfamiliar path, but you will need to make an important choice as to whether you proceed and follow where it leads. When faced with something outside the familiarity of a well-trod path and comfort zone, it can sometimes feel a little daunting. The Fool brings an unexpected opportunity into play, so you may need your sense of adventure and be prepared to take a risk.

In readings, the Fool suggests something completely new, which can prove helpful when someone is asking about their job or relationship, as the appearance frequently indicates something (or someone) stepping in that was entirely unanticipated and not already in the picture. In combinations, the Fool is easier to read when followed by another card (as shown in the following section) but can sometimes be quite challenging to interpret when it appears in the last position, since it represents a surprise.

Reversed or Badly Aspected

The more traditional aspect of folly; rash or immature behaviour, "rushing in where angels fear to tread." It can point to foolhardy or reckless behaviour through naivete or inexperience. Alternatively, it can show a lack of open-mindedness, an inability to embrace life with wonder, or being completely risk-averse.

Associations

Similar and Supporting Cards: All the Aces (new beginnings). In larger spreads, if the Fool and all four Aces appear collectively, it shows a completely new lifestyle with new beginnings across the board, a clean sweep. The High Priestess (the unknown factor).

Opposing and Contradictory Cards: Death or Ten of Swords (endings), the Hierophant (convention).

The Fool Featured Combinations

The Fool > Ace of Wands > the Empress: Surprise—an unexpected or unplanned pregnancy; take precautions if this isn't on your agenda!

Two of Wands > the Fool: Joining forces with others opens up a whole new avenue, discovering unanticipated potential to further explore, fledgling partnership in an unknown field (appropriate advice and guidance recommended).

The Fool > Three of Cups: Surprise party or celebration.

Seven of Cups > the Fool > the Tower: Take care to be realistic with a forthcoming choice, as naivete could lead you towards walking blindly into something that could be a disastrous move and backfire or blow up in your face—best to avoid; a highly disruptive situation.

The Fool > Knight of Cups: Surprise proposal or unexpected invitation.

The Fool > Six of Pentacles: Unanticipated gift or act of generosity.

The Fool > Eight of Pentacles: An unexpected opportunity for a new job or study placement; may originate from a surprising source.

The Fool > the Lovers: A blind date; the unexpected arrival of a love interest, perhaps from an unanticipated quarter.

The Fool > the Devil: A situation best avoided—this could lead to problems you may have difficulty extracting yourself from.

The Fool > Death: This could be a storm in a teacup that's over before it's really begun; a new beginning that goes nowhere or doesn't materialise. Whereas, in the opposite order…

Death > The Fool: …indicates major change and transformation: one door closes and another opens. The ending needs to take place in order to allow the unexpected new opportunity to enter.

Collectively, watch for: the Fool, High Priestess, Wheel of Fortune, Death, the Tower all appearing anywhere in a larger spread (such as the Life Spread and Anchor). All these cards suggest external factors outside the client's control coming into play and bringing enormous change that, while not necessarily bad (depending upon the ordering of other cards present), will be quite disruptive when it occurs.

I–THE MAGICIAN

Major Arcana (Trumps or Triumphs): Symbolic life experiences. Worldly affairs.

Flow: Quick

Polarity: Positive

Multiple Majors: Milestones and significant life events. Catalyst.

Keywords and Phrases: Mastery and skill. Initiating action.

Applied Meaning

In whatever context this card appears, the Magician encourages you to step forwards and take the initiative. It is time to be proactive, have confidence in your existing skills, and use talents to the best of your ability towards manifesting goals into reality.

Now is not the moment for hesitancy or self-doubt—if you take the first steps and put thought into action, you should discover that the journey is a work in progress. You don't need to have all the answers before you set off, as your natural talents will carry you through as you further develop capabilities towards mastery. The Magician is the reminder that you already hold all the potential you need within yourself and all the tools at your disposal, but you will need to focus your mind, direct your will, and take action.

When well-placed, this is a great card to help excel in work and study matters, as it shows innovative and creative thinking, focused and concentrated will, using the "power of now" to act effectively. It is particularly good for those involved in communications, media, writing, or speaking, or where those activities may be required.

Reversed or Badly Aspected

Can indicate swindling or trickery, manipulation, or misuse of abilities. Lack of willpower, loss of confidence or self-belief, self-doubt. Creative blocks, the inability to find expression, or misunderstandings and communication problems. Like quicksilver, it can point to a situation that swiftly becomes unpredictable.

Associations

Similar and Supporting Cards: Ace of Wands holds all the potential of active and creative energy; all Aces would be relevant with the Magician, as he offers the potentiality contained within each suit. The Chariot (confidence and drive), Three of Pentacles (mastery and skill), Two of Pentacles (dexterity).

Opposing and Contradictory Cards: The Devil (blocked energy), the Hanged Man (suspension, non-movement), Two of Swords (indecision, deadlock), Eight of Swords (restriction).

The Magician Featured Combinations

Ace of Wands > the Magician: Overlap of action drives this new project forwards; taking action but also being focused on the task can achieve mastery in your field. Can add some entrepreneurial flair if starting a new venture or business.

Seven of Wands > the Magician: Holding your own in negotiations; you will be able to effectively communicate your ideas and successfully move things forwards, probably in the direction you'd personally like to see them go.

The Magician > Eight of Wands: Speedy and productive communications which you may be initiating. Whereas...

Eight of Wands > the Magician: ...acting swiftly on news received will place you in a good position; strike whilst the iron is hot! (In either order, this pair of cards can also be a strong indication of the internet.)

Seven of Cups > the Magician: You're taking a proactive stance and can skilfully navigate through choices available to find the best option. Whereas, in the opposite order...

The Magician > Seven of Cups: ...using your initiative and some creative thinking can open up more options for you.

Eight of Cups > the Magician: Walking away is a wise move—it releases you from a situation that was draining your energy. Like clearing dead wood, renewed vitality and vision can be yours.

Two of Swords > the Magician > Eight of Swords: Indecision creates restriction and the inability to manifest desires. Creative ideas are blocked. Whereas...

Eight of Swords > the Magician: ...in this order, shows that it is within your power and ability to change a restrictive situation where you feel trapped; using an innovative approach and taking action can release you from it.

Three of Pentacles > the Magician: This is an excellent combination in relation to your main work; with an overlap in meaning of mastery, it shows you can forge ahead in your career. This would be a particularly good combination for those employed or engaged in communications, writing, or speaking.

*Watch for the Magician sandwiched or surrounded by: **Five of Swords, Page of Swords, the Moon, the Devil,** as it then takes on the negative aspect of the card: dishonest and hidden activity, trickery, cons or scams, manipulation, etc.

II–THE HIGH PRIESTESS

Major Arcana (Trumps or Triumphs): Symbolic life experiences. Worldly affairs.

Flow: Still

Polarity: Positive

Multiple Majors: Milestones and significant life events. Catalyst.

Keywords and Phrases: A mystery revealed. An enlightened moment that brings revelation. Intuition.

Applied Meaning

The High Priestess is the gatekeeper that guards the veil between the worlds, the wisdom and knowledge of universal mysteries. In readings, it can represent secret or hidden information becoming known to you that will be to your benefit. Although it is one of the secrecy cards, it has a more positive aspect that is able to reveal what the other cards have kept hidden. The difficulty with this card is that it is something of a conundrum to work with or open further. Since it references a secret, the High Priestess tends to keep it that way!

I have learnt from experience that this card can keep taking you round in a circle and, true to form of everything the card stands for, she will release the mystery on her own time, not ours. This is in a way similar to the Fool, in that if we knew what the surprise was, it would no longer be a surprise. However, what you can count on is that she will stay true to her word; hidden information will in some way come to light, a mystery will be revealed that will be helpful, or you will experience something of a revelation or "light bulb" moment. In the meantime, stay alert, but be still and wait.

Spiritual pursuits are favoured and would be especially relevant for those engaged in any form of psychic or spiritual work, or studying to gain wisdom and knowledge from higher concepts. The High Priestess encourages you to go within the stillness and listen to your subconscious through meditation, the language of your dreams, intuition, and your inner voice, allowing you to delve deeper to awaken and develop spiritual awareness and your unexplored or unfulfilled potential.

Reversed or Badly Aspected

Superficial knowledge, misuse of ability, blocked energy, switched off from reality. Alternatively, it can signal reemerging after a period of isolation.

Associations

Similar and Supporting Cards: The High Priestess has an enigmatic quality that makes it similar, yet different, to a number of cards. Perhaps because of her mysterious complexity, the nature is experienced slightly differently and can be difficult to pin down. For instance, quiet reflection and contemplation brings wisdom from **the Hermit. The Hierophant** is also a wise teacher but dispenses guidance and information more openly. **The Fool** (unknown factor). **The Magician** accentuates psychic ability, as can **the Moon**, but the latter can also be an opposing card, depending upon how it is aspected.

Opposing and Contradictory Cards: The Moon, **the Devil**, and **Five of Swords** also have aspects of secrecy and hidden information but are experienced differently and less favourably. **The Empress** (potential fulfilled, "mother" of the earthly domain).

The High Priestess Featured Combinations

Ace of Wands > High Priestess: A new mind-body-spirit business, job, or project; hidden information coming to light that will help as you move forwards.

Two of Wands > High Priestess: May feel you're working blind initially but helpful information will come to light; a revelation on the path ahead.

Three of Wands > the High Priestess: Expansion and delving deeper into unknown areas, helpful information will be revealed as you progress. Commercial business or trade of a metaphysical or spiritual nature.

Seven of Cups > the High Priestess: You may feel in a quandary and uncertain what to do; try to delay making any decision for the moment as you don't yet have the full picture. Some important information will be made known to you and then you will understand how to proceed.

Five of Swords > the High Priestess > Ace of Swords: Outfoxing the fox. Information will come to light that works to your advantage and allows you to triumph; it could be with regards to a smear campaign or some kind of skulduggery against you.

Eight of Pentacles > the High Priestess: May suggest a course of study in metaphysical or esoteric subjects. In the opposite order …

The High Priestess > Eight of Pentacles: … stay alert for incoming information on the grapevine that can lead to a new job or work.

The High Priestess > the Fool: This is one of the trickiest combinations— you're working with completely unknown aspects, but it is easier to read in this order: Something will become known to you that opens up a completely new and unfamiliar pathway. Whereas, in the opposite order …

The Fool > the High Priestess: …you are working blind. It could be surprising information that will come to light in a completely unexpected way; however, it can also point to setting off in a new direction that is not only outside the usual comfort zone but will rely on instinct and require blind faith.

The High Priestess > the Magician > the Moon: When these three cards appear together, it can often be an indication of psychic abilities or involvement and encourages developing intuitive gifts further; the Magician accentuates psychic gifts.

The High Priestess > the Lovers: This combination can indicate a secret admirer who will soon be revealed. (The cards following, if applicable, will show where it leads.)

The High Priestess > the Moon > the Devil: Can indicate misuse of psychic gifts and abilities, delving into the wrong areas. Triple whammy of secrecy represented and reinforced where the High Priestess is blocked.

III–THE EMPRESS

Major Arcana (Trumps or Triumphs): Symbolic life experiences. Worldly affairs.

Flow: Steady

Polarity: Positive

Multiple Majors: Milestones and significant life events. Catalyst.

Keywords and Phrases: Fruitful abundance, bountiful. Fertility. Motherhood (parenting). Nurturing.

Applied Meaning

The Empress brings the fruitful and abundant harvest, so things that have been ripening now come to fruition. This is an excellent card for all situations but is particularly favoured regarding family, harmonious relationships, and emotional and financial security.

As the female archetype, this is also the main card we look for in relation to fertility matters, children, motherhood, and parenting. The "mothering" aspect translates into nurturing whether with relationships or projects, applying care and attention so matters can blossom and bloom. The only aspect to watch for is when it is negatively influenced by surrounding cards, which in certain circumstances may suggest smothering.

Although the court cards are the main indicators for people rather than the majors, the Empress is often an exception as it can point to the mother. This may be due to the amount of influence from the mother figure in formative years, whether for good or bad. Situations concerning the mother are often shown with this card and are quite reliable in this regard. A woman who holds a powerful rank or position can sometimes be indicated.

Beautifying the home and surroundings can feature in the form of creativity, art, and luxury items. But whilst trying to create beautiful and harmonious environments for others, it reminds you to also take time for some tender loving care and pampering for yourself as well.

Reversed or Badly Aspected

Can indicate fertility problems, difficulty with a mother figure or one who dominates, domestic issues, over-giving or excessive smothering, extravagance, vanity, creative blocks.

Associations

Similar and Supporting Cards: **Seven of Pentacles** (gathering your harvest), **Nine of Pentacles** (abundance), **Ten of Pentacles** (home and family), **Ten of Cups** (happy marriage and family life), **Temperance** (harmonious balance). Strengthens other indications when appearing with marriage and relationship cards.

Opposing and Contradictory Cards: **The Emperor** is the male yang to the female yin, in that opposite forces also complement one another.

Four of Pentacles (withholding), Five of Pentacles (scarcity), the High Priestess (unfulfilled potential), the Devil (unhealthy).

The Empress Featured Combinations

Ace of Wands > the Empress: Usually conception and pregnancy but sometimes birth (in either order); may also be joined by the Ace of Cups (usually for the birth). In the work area of a spread, new venture will be successful if you nurture it.

Three of Wands > the Empress: A successful plan for parenthood, family planning and expanding your brood. In other matters, building upon success and reaping abundant rewards from earlier progress and gains.

Nine of Wands > the Empress: With perseverance and careful attention your plans will flourish and pay off abundantly.

The Empress > Ten of Wands: Feeling overwhelmed with parenting responsibilities or fertility pressure. Can represent an overbearing mother figure or "smother love." When the following also appear ...

The Lovers > the Empress > Ten of Wands: ...can show a relationship that constantly needs bolstering or even "overkill" (the smothering aspect). The Lovers and the Empress as a pair or closing a sequence would suggest a blossoming relationship, but the Ten of Wands following leads into more negative territory, suggesting the burden or overwhelm that lies ahead as a consequence.

Ten of Cups > the Empress: Happy marriage and family life are bolstered with the presence of the Empress; plans come to fruition and everything blossoms with abundance, bringing great happiness for all concerned.

Nine of Pentacles > the Empress: Financial abundance; can indicate luxury items, but an extremely bountiful and fortunate pairing.

Ten of Pentacles > Judgement > the Empress: Home renovations, refurbishing and beautifying, most particularly interiors.

The Empress > the Emperor: Can represent a power couple involved (distinct from your court cards); occasionally the parents although not usually, unless they are powerful public figures or highly successful, such as: royalty, politicians, celebrities, or of material high status.

The Hierophant > the Empress: Check for institutions connected to children, such as hospitals (maternity, paediatrics, or gynaecology), kindergartens, or primary schools.

The Empress > the Devil: This combination can suggest the domineering influence of an important woman that can be suffocating.

Collectively, watch for: the High Priestess, the Empress, and the Moon appearing together in a reading, as they can indicate a strong and powerful female influence; women's mysteries. Strength can also add to feminine power.

IV–THE EMPEROR

Major Arcana (Trumps or Triumphs): Symbolic life experiences. Worldly affairs.

Flow: Steady

Polarity: Positive

Multiple Majors: Milestones and significant life events. Catalyst.

Keywords and Phrases: Leadership. Authority. Ambition. Stability.

Applied Meaning

The Emperor encompasses the traditional male archetype and those qualities associated with it, so it is a card of leadership, ambition, authority, and provides an orderly stabilising effect to matters. In a reading it can show the need to rise to the challenge with a calm head and cool rationale; it may be time to step up to the plate and take responsibility to do whatever needs to be done. On a personal level, the Emperor encourages you to be confident, assertive, and reclaim your power.

In work and business, it places you in a powerful position to achieve your goals and realise your ambitions. Others may look to you for direction and guidance; with the right cards, it can suggest a promotion, a role of responsibility or leadership, an authority in your field, or being the boss.

On the home front, you may be viewed as the breadwinner and protector of your clan, the benevolent leader of your pack and domain, establishing boundaries and taking care of practicalities. In relationships, it may signal the need for a head-over-heart approach and the use of strong reasoning. It can also bring more stability to the partnership.

Whilst the court cards are used as the main indicators for people, the Emperor can sometimes represent a powerful man, though in this respect I tend to find it acts as a representation of higher authority figures in positions of power, usually the leaders and rule makers who create structure and bring order to our societies and in the wider world. The card can also feature closer to home to represent a strong father figure or influential male figure.

Reversed or Badly Aspected

A domineering, aggressive, or bullying influence, tyrant, or dictator, abuse of power. Instability, failed ambitions, weakened authority or position.

Associations

Similar and Supporting Cards: The Magician (proactive and confident), **Justice** (logic and reason), **the Hierophant** (tradition and structure), **the Chariot** (focused will and drive), **Ace of Swords** (force of strength and power), **Four of Wands**, and **Ten of Pentacles** (the stability aspect).

Opposing and Contradictory Cards: Four of Cups (apathy), **the Fool,** (spontaneity), **Temperance** (gentle diplomacy and moderation). **The Empress** is the female yin to the yang of the Emperor, where the opposite forces are complementary to one another.

The Emperor Featured Combinations

Ace of Wands > the Emperor: A new role with a position of authority or could lead to promotion. Stepping up to take control and handle responsibilities in a new venture will bring success.

Three of Wands > the Emperor > Eight of Swords: Progress and expansion in the short term brings stability, but be careful you're not being overambitious, overreaching, or moving too quickly, as there will be restrictions further down the road and they could possibly be self-inflicted.

Five of Wands > the Emperor: Taking command and restoring order from chaos to bring a sense of stability to the situation.

Six of Wands > the Emperor: Getting the "top job," promotion to a senior or top position.

Five of Cups > the Emperor: Stiff upper lip, dealing with disappointment in a cool and rational manner, not wearing your heart on your sleeve.

Seven of Cups > the Emperor: Grasping the nettle, taking control and being decisive with a realistic attitude about options and choices. (If available, a card preceding the Seven would help provide clarification over what the options relate to.)

The Emperor > the Chariot > Three of Swords: If you go hurtling into this in a single-minded and heavy-handed manner, it will cause upsets with others.

Three of Pentacles > the Emperor > Ten of Wands: Under pressure from the boss or authority figures at work. Taking on a more responsible position and finding it too much—executive stress.

Four of Pentacles > Nine of Wands > the Emperor: You're prepared to do whatever it takes and work hard towards material goals; you can make this happen, but don't lose sight of your EQ (emotional intelligence) in the process.

The Magician > the Chariot > the Emperor: Full steam ahead with strong decisive action. A powerhouse of energy, this powerful trio of majors shows a natural progression of events through proactive and focussed effort, being single-minded whilst harnessing abilities to push forwards towards a successful outcome.

The Emperor > Temperance: The iron fist in the velvet glove; moderating your approach and using diplomacy can help soften the edges to bring about the desired outcome.

The Emperor > the Devil: Can be indications of bullying, the domineering boss, or abuse of power by one in authority or position of responsibility.

V–The Hierophant

Major Arcana (Trumps or Triumphs): Symbolic life experiences. Worldly affairs.

Flow: Steady

Polarity: Positive

Multiple Majors: Milestones and significant life events. Catalyst.

Keywords and Phrases: Traditional values. Institutions. "The Establishment." Marriage. Ethics and morals.

Applied Meaning

Of all the cards, this is the one that most students seem to struggle with and causes confusion as to what it means to them. The concept of the card is perhaps slightly lost in our society of today, as it hearkens back to a time when the church and organised religion held more power over the majority of the populace.

The Hierophant is the archetype for traditional values, following or conforming to accepted social and cultural norms, and it often represents some form of institution. There are occasions when it can represent the church or a religious establishment, for example, a church wedding or ceremony, but also the institution of marriage, or the traditional role and social institution of the family.

Large organisations can also feature, usually those that follow set rules and procedures that are not easily open to change or of a bureaucratic nature, such as government departments and officials, hospitals, formal educational facilities, the church, charities, or nonprofits. Sometimes it can represent large companies or corporations as well, due to their structure and layers, which often affect the speed with which they are able to activate change. Long-standing traditional family companies may fall under this umbrella too.

The Hierophant can indicate a wise and trusted person who can provide good guidance, a teacher, mentor, or someone with recognised standing in your community. As a card of convention, it has a conservative nature and advises you to act with good morals and within guiding principles, to follow the rules and do the right thing to meet certain expectations, or to follow an established path rather than being innovative and colouring outside the lines at this time.

In combinations, the surrounding and supporting cards can help provide direction as to which way to apply the meanings of the card.

Reversed or Badly Aspected

Dogmatic, indoctrination, corrupt officials, a self-serving teacher or mentor, lack of moral principles, unorthodoxy, loss of faith.

Associations

Similar and Supporting Cards: The Hermit (wisdom), **Ten of Pentacles** (family). When appearing together with other marriage cards, it would support and strengthen the association, such as: **Ten of Cups, the Lovers, Two of Cups, Four of Wands, Three of Cups, Justice, Ace of Pentacles**.

There are numerous combinations that can indicate marriage, as we have already seen, but the ordering and flow of cards is usually the determining factor, when reading in a simple line from left to right.

Opposing and Contradictory: The Fool (free spirit, adventurous), **the Hanged Man** (unconventional, lateral thinking), **the Devil** (not following moral codes).

The Hierophant is a partner card and other side of the coin in relation to both **the High Priestess** and **the Emperor**. The High Priestess is knowledge of the secret mysteries, the internal unfolding of connection with the Divine, whereas the Hierophant is the external and recognised official source of teaching moral principle. In previous times, the Emperor represented secular rule, whilst the Hierophant (or Le Pape) symbolised religious authority.

The Hierophant Featured Combinations

The Hierophant > Four of Pentacles: Banks and loan institutions.

The Hierophant > Six of Pentacles: Charitable foundations and institutions.

The Hierophant > Eight of Pentacles: University and formal education facilities (the Hermit may also feature). Similarly ...

The Hierophant > Eight of Pentacles > Six of Wands: ... graduation from a recognised educational establishment.

The Hierophant > Ten of Pentacles: Traditional institution of the family. Also ...

Three of Pentacles > the Hierophant > Ten of Pentacles: ... working in the family business or working for a long-standing and traditional family company.

Two of Cups > the Hierophant > Ten of Cups: Institution of marriage. Also ...

Two of Cups > the Hierophant > Three of Cups: ... a marriage ceremony and wedding breakfast/celebration. (The Lovers may sometimes appear instead of the Two of Cups.)

Page of Cups > the Hierophant > Three of Cups: Religious ceremony and celebration for a child, such as a baptism or naming ceremony, confirmation, bar or bat mitzvah, etc. (As a card of tradition, the

Hierophant covers all different faiths and religions.) Can also indicate messages concerning a religious ceremony.

Temperance > the Hierophant > the Star: Hospitals and places of healing. Also ...

Eight of Swords > the Hierophant > Four of Swords: ... hospital confinement and convalescence (ordering can differ).

The Hierophant > the Hermit: Receiving wise guidance and knowledge from a teacher and mentor.

Death > the Hierophant > Five of Cups: Funeral ceremony and mourning.

The Devil > the Hierophant: Taking the moral high ground, acting on higher ethics and values to do the right thing. Whereas, in the opposite order ...

The Hierophant > the Devil: ... may indicate a corrupt organisation or official. Also ...

The Devil > the Hierophant > Five of Swords: ... can indicate a dodgy organisation or hidden corruption within an institution (note how the card is sandwiched, providing a stronger indication).

VI–THE LOVERS

Major Arcana (Trumps or Triumphs): Symbolic life experiences. Worldly affairs.

Flow: Flowing

Polarity: Positive

Multiple Majors: Milestones and significant life events. Catalyst.

Keywords and Phrases: Love relationship, romance.

Applied Meaning

The Lovers represents a love relationship, union, partnership, or marriage, depending upon the setting. For those who are single, it can show a new love interest, an attraction, and the potential for a new relationship entering the scene. For those happily attached, it represents their existing partnership rather than another one arriving, or the involvement of their partner in connection to the situation being shown. When couples combine their lives they usually operate as a joint entity rather than independently, since their actions affect each other. Attached people sometimes worry that the card indicates a love triangle, but this would be shown by the influence of the appropriate negative surrounding cards.

Some see this card as one of choice, but early roots indicate it was the Trump or Triumph of Love before the concept of a choice between vice or virtue was introduced, and Waite returned to the original interpretation. As my reading style is fairly precise for divination and predictive purposes, I tend to focus upon the Seven of Cups as the main card for choices, whilst business partnerships or collaborations would be indicated by the Two of Wands, leaving the Lovers free for love and romance.

Similarly, if the Lovers appeared in connection to work or questions concerning career, it would still indicate the involvement or influence of a love relationship rather than a love of work. Quite a lot of people meet a partner through their work environment; some couples work or go into business together, a partner can introduce a valuable lead or opening, many people consult with their partner over work matters, and many receive their partner's support in a tricky situation at work, as just some examples.

Reversed or Badly Aspected

Relationship problems and lack of harmony, incompatibility, unfulfilled romantic expectations, loveless union, unrequited or unreciprocated love, separation or without relationship.

Associations

Similar and Supporting Cards: Ace of Cups (new relationship), Two of Cups (loving union). It would also support other marriage and commitment cards and all marriage combinations, such as: Two, Three, and Ten of Cups, Four of Wands, the Hierophant.

Opposing and Contradictory Cards: The Devil (unhealthy, tainted), **Four of Cups** (dispassionate), **Five of Cups** (sadness), **Three of Swords** (stormy emotions). **Four of Swords** and **the Hermit** (withdrawal, aloneness)

The Lovers Featured Combinations

For relationships, this is one of the easiest cards to work with, particularly when followed by another card, as it shows the direction things will take. This is also one of the areas that is most often asked about in readings, so I have included an extended selection. Some of the most popular combinations may be repeats from other pages to save you from having to cross-reference, but there are still others featured on other card pages as it is too extensive to list them all.

The Lovers > Ace of Cups: Love attraction and a new relationship beginning.

The Lovers > Two of Cups: The deepening bond of a love relationship moving to the next stage. In the opposite order...

Two of Cups > the Lovers: ...can show romance developing with someone already known (if single), most particularly when the Ace of Cups is absent, which usually shows the start of a new relationship.

The Lovers > Five of Cups: Needs little by way of explanation—heartbreak, upset and tears, but check the following cards or other indications, as the Five has a temporary influence and can often be just a minor blip.

The Lovers > Five of Cups > Ten of Swords: For confirmation of an ending I would prefer to see the Ten of Swords or Death immediately following. Whereas...

The Lovers > Five of Cups > Temperance: ...would show an upset but healing and renewal following, found through compromise and mediation. **Judgement** would also show reconciliation (also see below).

Six of Cups > the Lovers: The potential of a relationship with someone from the past; it could be an old flame or former attraction but not necessarily someone previously romantically involved with, just that there is a past connection with the person. Also...

Judgement > the Lovers: ... this is the main combination I look for to indicate the resurrection and revival of an old relationship or reconciliation (can appear in the opposite order too).

Knight of Cups > the Lovers: A romantic offer or proposal of involvement, or an invitation for a date (the **Ace of Cups** can sometimes replace the Lovers).

The Lovers > Knight of Cups > the Hierophant: Can be a marriage proposal. (Also see **Two of Cups**, page 70 and **Ten of Cups**, page 94 for more marriage combinations.)

The Lovers > Ten of Cups: Potential for a relationship to become serious fairly quickly, as we're moving straight to the Ten, most particularly if lower cards are absent (Ace or Two of Cups, for instance). For those already dating, it suggests a commitment being made and the relationship becoming more permanent, e.g., marriage, although in larger spreads there would usually be additional marriage cards on the table. For those attached, complete happiness and contentment with the partner and family life.

Two of Wands > the Lovers: Partners in work and love; a business partnership with (or involving) your significant other. If single, a work collaboration could lead to romance.

The Lovers > Four of Wands: Can be a romantic weekend, particularly if other travel cards are present in the combination. A relationship becoming more stable.

Three of Swords > the Lovers: Long-distance relationships are often indicated with this combination. In the opposite order ...

The Lovers > Three of Swords: ... it would show stormy emotions, upsets, and quarrels; check the following card to see if things escalate or remain minor.

Five of Swords > the Lovers > the Devil > the Moon: When found in full combination with these three cards in any order surrounding the Lovers, something is definitely amiss and may be cause for concern, unless it comes at the end as the last card of the group.

Three of Pentacles > the Lovers: Romantic attraction through your main work. If attached, you could be putting your head together with a partner in relation to something concerning your main area of work; their influence will be important to you in some way regarding a work matter.

The Fool > the Lovers: For singles, it can be a blind date or a surprise relationship from an unexpected source. With the Fool, it normally indicates someone completely new, rather than known already.

The Lovers > the Devil: Not a good sign for a healthy or long-term relationship.

The Lovers > the Hierophant > the Devil: Watch for this one when hovering around an attraction (or the relevant corresponding court card for the person instead)—it can indicate someone who is already married. Whereas ...

The Lovers > the Hierophant > Ten of Cups: ... would be an indication of marriage (also see the **Two of Cups**, page 70 and **Ten of Cups**, page 94 for more combinations).

VII–The Chariot

Major Arcana (Trumps or Triumphs): Symbolic life experiences. Worldly affairs.

Flow: Brisk pace

Polarity: Positive

Multiple Majors: Milestones and significant life events. Catalyst.

Keywords and Phrases: Triumph over obstacles. Willpower. Journey.

Applied Meaning

The Chariot represents victory and triumph through exerting and controlling your will in the direction of your goals, so it is quite a forceful card. Generally, it is a good omen for success, although not usually without some effort—but with the right approach, obstacles can be overcome and to the victor go the spoils!

In whichever area of life it may appear, it advises to plot your course and then throw everything you have behind it to literally drive things through. You need to be determined with an unwavering focus and self-discipline, to harness and control the energy rather than allowing it to become scattered, as a chariot pulled in opposing directions would topple over.

In the Magician, we speak of mastering the will and initiating action; with the Chariot, we reach the effect and outcome of exerting that will, the external manifestation and resulting victory for those efforts brought into being.

As a mode of transport, the Chariot can also signify a journey, particularly when supported by other travel cards. The pace is brisk, so it can indicate a quick trip or one by road and over land that would feature enclosed or wheeled vehicles, such as a car, bus, train, caravan, or motor-home. On a mundane level, it may reference a situation involving your car.

Reversed or Badly Aspected

A loss of focus, being weak-willed, inability to follow through, falling at the last hurdle, defeat, or failure of plans. It can also point to travel snarl-ups or vehicle problems.

Associations

    Similar and Supporting Cards: Ace of Swords (triumph over adversity) and any success cards would be relevant, **the World**, etc. **Knight of Swords** (speed and decisive action), **the Magician** (focused thought), **the Emperor** (taking control), **Six of Wands** and **the Star** (acclaim). **Eight of Wands, Knight of Wands, Six of Swords** would strengthen the association with travel.

    Opposing and Contradictory Cards: Any cards indicating defeat or failure, such as the **Ten of Swords** and similar. **The Hanged Man** and **Two of Swords** (lack of movement), **Four of Cups** (apathy). **Strength** is similar but opposite, in that the element of control is expressed differently; these two often appear together, but Strength indicates inner power and with the Chariot becomes externalised. This is a complementary pair similar to the Empress and Emperor. Also, the **Knight of Pentacles** would finally bring a result but takes a long time and in a quieter fashion, so not with the speed or fanfares of the Chariot.

The Chariot Featured Combinations

Ace of Wands > the Chariot: Taking control of a new venture and steaming ahead with determination. Runaway project and instant hit; lots of speed and energy with this one.

Two of Wands > the Chariot: An early win if you can harness good self-discipline, triumph over any short-term obstacles. With all parties pulling in the right direction, a working partnership has good prospects to succeed.

Three of Wands > the Chariot: On a commercial basis, road haulage and land freight can be indicated. Capitalising on earlier success will bring a greater reward if you stay determined and focused.

The Chariot > Four of Wands: Road trip and short break.

Ace of Cups > the Chariot: New relationship going well and taking off with gusto. For those more settled, a new beginning brings happiness for all concerned that works out well and is a resounding success.

The Chariot > Ace of Pentacles: On a mundane level, can be car or vehicle documents, contract for a new car, travel ticket, or associated documents.

The Chariot > Eight of Pentacles: Can be driving lessons. In work matters, determination and drive successfully bring new work for you. In the opposite order ...

Eight of Pentacles > the Chariot: ... can show new work taking off fairly rapidly. You can do really well once you have mastered the basics and put the finishing touches in place. These two cards balance each other out well; Pentacles temper the forthright energy.

The Chariot > Ten of Swords: Crash-and-burn scenario, could be too much too soon but it's heading for failure. Whereas, in the opposite order ...

Ten of Swords > the Chariot: … great resilience to bounce back and charge forwards from a disappointment, which will bring triumph after a previous failure.

Knight of Swords > the Chariot: Hot to trot and raring to go, enormous speed and energy indicated; taking speedy and decisive action. Possibly an urgent journey.

The Chariot > the Emperor > the Hermit: Dealing with this matter too forcefully could leave you feeling isolated as a result; take time to contemplate logistics and prospective outcomes. Preferably, we wish to see something to soften the edges and add a more diplomatic approach, such as: **The Chariot > the Emperor > Temperance**.

The World > the Chariot: International travel can be indicated. Depending upon context, can also be an indicator of triumph and success, although in the opposite order would show a natural progression, such as **the Chariot > the World**.

VIII–STRENGTH

Major Arcana (Trumps or Triumphs): Symbolic life experiences. Worldly affairs.

Flow: Steady pace

Polarity: Positive

Multiple Majors: Milestones and significant life events. Catalyst.

Keywords and Phrases: Inner strength and courage. Resolve. Fortitude. Tenacity. Endurance.

Applied Meaning

The Strength card refers to inner strength and qualities associated with it, such as quiet determination, patience, and resolve rather than forceful action or aggressive tendencies. When this card appears in a reading, it often points to a situation that may require tenacity and endurance, not in the sense of suffering but of resilience, possibly in terms of the long haul; a marathon rather than a sprint.

You may be dealing with a challenging situation that requires you to dig deep and draw upon your inner reserves, but you can do so with dignity and good grace. With gentle persuasion, diplomacy, and a gentle touch, you can bring others around to your way of thinking and perhaps even charm the proverbial birds from the trees. Above all, you have your eye on the long game, not the short-term fix. I like to think of this card as the understatement; people could underestimate you but in a way that can work to your advantage. That's not to say this is in any way a card of malicious intent, but it can pack quite a punch if you can utilise the message it provides.

The lion can be representative of inner courage, the quiet still voice that holds the line, steely and resolute even when under pressure. For some, the lion represents taming one's own inner animal instincts and keeping them under control, but in other quarters, it can add a certain magnetism to relationships and suggest underlying passions.

Reversed or Badly Aspected

Lack of backbone, weakened resolve, loss of self-belief, inability to be able to see something through, though not necessarily through a personal failing, martyrdom, forceful, unrestrained, overstatement, or going overboard.

Associations

Similar and Supporting Cards: Nine of Wands (perseverance), **Seven of Wands** (holding firm), **Ace of Swords** (ability to overcome), **Seven** and **Knight of Pentacles** (slow and steady, long-term), **Temperance** (patience and diplomacy).

Opposing and Contradictory Cards: Four of Cups (apathy), **the Devil** (excess), fast moving cards, such as: **Eight of Wands** and **Knight of Swords**. **The Chariot** is similar but opposing with its outward and more forceful expression.

Strength Featured Combinations

Five of Wands > Strength: Rising to the challenge, your resolute and dogged determination will see you through any petty obstacles that may arise. Can also show rising above and sailing past competitive forces to win the day.

Seven of Wands > Strength: Holding steady and digging in, you feel strongly about something and are prepared to see it through with great resolve.

Strength > Ten of Wands: Despite best efforts, this may feel as though it proves too much to continue: an uphill struggle that could get the better of you. Whereas, in the opposite order...

Ten of Wands > Strength: ... can mean feeling under pressure but battling on and dealing with everything in a calm, collected way to get to where you need to be. May feel like an endurance test, but you can handle it.

Strength > Eight of Cups: Although you start out with good intentions, they could wear thin after a while and lead to abandoning the matter. Sometimes strength is also knowing when to execute an exit strategy.

Three of Swords > Strength: Diplomacy and the art of gentle persuasion can cool harsh words and alleviate stormy upsets.

Seven of Swords > Strength: A long-term strategy; take an extremely careful approach armed with diplomacy and a charm offensive.

Eight of Swords > Strength > Nine of Swords: Enduring a difficult situation but resolve is weakened; possibly a lack of self-belief (trapped card).

Three of Pentacles > Four of Pentacles > Strength: Working hard towards long-term career goals, you're prepared to put in the effort and have the determination to see it through.

Strength > Seven of Pentacles: This may take a while, but long-term efforts will be rewarded and bear fruit.

Strength > the Chariot > Ace of Swords: Inner and outer resolve will be needed to overcome challenges or setbacks, but you will be successful in your aims. This powerful trio is like throwing every ounce of energy you have at something and shows an enormous amount of determination to bring about a triumphant conclusion.

The Tower > Strength: You are made of sterner stuff; having inner courage and tenacity through the eye of the storm, you have the ability to pick yourself up and dust yourself off to take things in your stride. Others may view you as unfazed or unruffled and in control after a disruptive situation. Weathering the storm and enduring whatever life throws at you.

IX–THE HERMIT

Major Arcana (Trumps or Triumphs): Symbolic life experiences. Worldly affairs.

Flow: Slow

Polarity: Neutral/Positive

Multiple Majors: Milestones and significant life events. Catalyst.

Keywords and Phrases: Contemplation. Wisdom and maturity. Prudence.

Applied Meaning

When the Hermit appears in a reading, it can indicate that a period of quiet thought and introspection may be required in order to contemplate the deeper aspects of a situation. This is a card of turning inward, meditating, and listening to the self rather than looking to external factors for the answer, usually suggesting that you already know the answer but just need some quiet time to access it. Withdrawing and removing yourself from the noise and "busyness" of life may be favoured at this time, allowing you to really listen and be guided by the wisdom of your inner voice.

This is an excellent card for fact-finding, research, and generally gathering wisdom and information, making it favourable when appearing alongside learning, teaching, or educational cards. It can recommend a cautious and prudent approach to matters, taking time to do your homework, background checks, and thinking things through carefully. Nothing is rushed with this card, and it has the slow-moving element of age and time, suggesting wisdom or matters reaching maturity in the fullness of time.

You may not feel particularly sociable at the moment and prefer solitary pursuits and pulling back from the madding crowd. It can signify a time of solitude and withdrawal, although it tends to suggest aloneness rather than being lonely.

Reversed or Badly Aspected

Can point to a lack of maturity or rash behaviour, although it often intensifies the solitary into a more negative aspect, such as isolation. The slow-moving element of the card transforms into obstacles and delays. May suggest problems with an older person.

Associations

Similar and Supporting Cards: Varying qualities dependent upon how it is aspected, **Four of Swords** (withdrawal), **Four of Pentacles** (caution), **Eight of Pentacles** (learning), **the High Priestess** (deeper knowledge), **the Hierophant** (wise teacher or mentor), **Temperance** (patience). Whilst **the Hanged Man** can have a delaying effect, it is also the card of alternative thinking—cards that slow down the pace, such as **the Knight of Pentacles**, would reinforce this aspect.

Opposing and Contradictory Cards: Two of Wands (working partnerships or collaborations), **Three of Cups** (or any cards suggesting group activity), **Seven of Cups** (daydreams), **the Fool** (carefree spirit). **The Moon** (clouded thought). All fast-moving cards: **Eight of Wands**, **Knight of Swords**, etc.

The Hermit Featured Combinations

Ace of Wands > the Hermit: New ventures progress slowly after initial buzz, take a cautious approach and seek wise counsel in order to progress.

The Hermit > Ten of Wands: Overthinking or overanalysing creates its own burden. If this combination is also followed by **the Two of Swords** ...

The Hermit > Ten of Wands > Two of Swords: ... it would add indecision and result in no progress or further movement.

Five of Cups > the Hermit: Taking time out to heal hurts after an emotional upset, withdrawing to lick your wounds and contemplate next steps.

Knight of Cups > the Hermit: Whatever is being offered provides food for thought; you may be doing due diligence and fact-checking before continuing. (A card preceding the Knight would indicate the nature of the offer.)

Three of Swords > the Hermit > Two of Swords: Withdrawal after a quarrel leads to a standoff.

Knight of Pentacles > Seven of Pentacles > the Hermit: Long-term investments reaching maturity through careful and considered planning. (The Hermit and Knight can appear on either side of the Seven.)

The Hermit > the Fool: Taking time to consider before embarking upon an entirely new path. May suggest throwing caution to the wind.

The Chariot > the Hermit: Slamming on the brakes; something that has been hurtling along and you were forcefully pushing needs to slow down and will require careful thought as you move forwards.

The Hierophant > Eight of Pentacles > the Hermit: Learning and studying; gathering wisdom in an educational institution or setting (can be in any order).

The Hermit > the Moon > Eight of Swords: Clouded and confused thinking leads to restriction or becoming trapped within your own thoughts. Whereas ...

The Moon > the Hermit: ... indicates taking your time and cutting through illusion with a wise and prudent approach—or, gathering information (a good counterbalance when following **the Moon** or **Seven of Cups**).

X–WHEEL OF FORTUNE

Major Arcana (Trumps or Triumphs): Symbolic life experiences. Worldly affairs.

Flow: Continuous movement

Polarity: Usually positive

Multiple Majors: Milestones and significant life events. Catalyst.

Keywords and Phrases: Cycle change. Luck and destiny. Fate and fortune.

Applied Meaning

As the name implies, the Wheel is the card of luck and reflects our fortunes, for good or ill, although it is usually of the positive variety and for the most part represents good luck and good fortune. Lady Luck and the hand of fate turn the Wheel, bringing change in the ever-moving cycle of life, but fate can be a fickle friend and not one who can be relied upon … such is the nature of luck.

This is one of the cards for which I would consider external factors; we have little control over the events that are brought into play, as they are often circumstances beyond and outside of our control (others noted below). We do what we can with all the tools available at our disposal, but sometimes it is that little bit of luck that puts the wind in our sails to help make the difference. The Wheel of Fortune signifies when luck is running in your favour.

When the Wheel appears in your reading, it signals a change of cycle on the horizon when fortunate opportunities will open up. It is a time to make the most of the favourable influences it brings, for we never know when the Wheel will turn again—such is the transient nature of change. In early versions of the card, the goddess Fortuna turns the handle of the Wheel with various figures positioned at four different points of the rim, raising them up or casting them down as it spins, as their fortunes rise and fall in response.

In combinations, pay particular attention to the card that follows, which helps to indicate which way luck is heading. If the Wheel is found at the end of a line, or with no further card following, we can at least see that change is on the horizon and usually of a positive persuasion. Although the Wheel often presents itself in turnaround situations where it indicates a swift cycle change from one extreme to the other, sometimes it can be more literal and suggest something going round in a circle.

Reversed or Badly Aspected

Can indicate a run of bad luck, luck running out, or a misfortune. For some it still retains the positive influence though to a lesser extent or where matters are delayed.

Associations

> **Similar and Supporting Cards:** Together with **multiple Sevens** in the reading indicates a cycle change. **Death** (major change). Positive cards would back up the fortunate influence: **Nine of Cups**, **the Sun**, etc.

Opposing and Contradictory Cards: The Hanged Man (non-movement). **The Tower** (misfortune).

Wheel of Fortune Featured Combinations

Ace of Wands > Wheel of Fortune: A fortunate endeavour; maximise a window of opportunity that can bring positive change (check card following to see where it leads.) In the opposite order …

Wheel of Fortune > Ace of Wands: … may point to a lucky break that opens up an exciting new avenue.

Knight of Wands > Ten of Swords > Wheel of Fortune > Judgement: This one is familiar in property sales or moves, where the transaction falls through but then fortuitous circumstances bring it back round again to be revived.

Two of Cups > Wheel of Fortune: Lucky in love, a fortunate match. And …

The Hierophant > Ten of Cups > Wheel of Fortune: … if present with marriage cards, it can show a fortunate pairing or the changing circumstances of literally marrying two fortunes together.

Wheel of Fortune > Three of Cups: Celebrating your good fortune with friends and family. In either order, it can also represent a social event at a casino or a place where speculation is entertainment (racetrack, etc.).

Five of Pentacles > Wheel of Fortune > Nine of Pentacles: Earlier losses regained; a stroke of good fortune sees a turnaround in financial affairs. Whereas …

Wheel of Fortune > Five of Pentacles: … could be a gamble that does not pay off; more commonly points to an unfavourable change in financial fortunes.

Nine of Swords > Ten of Wands > Wheel of Fortune: Change is coming and matters will improve—hang on tight, as there will be an opportunity to turn things around. (The Wheel at the end releases the negative cycle.)

Wheel of Fortune > the Devil: Can indicate speculation habit or gambling addiction.

The Sun > Wheel of Fortune > the World: These three together (in any order) bring good fortune and success to a larger degree than your usual experience. If **the Star** is also included, it may put you in the spotlight, with fame of some description.

XI–JUSTICE

Major Arcana (Trumps or Triumphs): Symbolic life experiences. Worldly affairs.

Flow: Steady

Polarity: Neutral/Positive

Multiple Majors: Milestones and significant life events. Catalyst.

Keywords and Phrases: Legal matters. Balanced thought, impartiality.

Applied Meaning

The Justice card can highlight anything of a legal nature, from straightforwards contracts and agreements to court matters. Legal aspects are quite common-place in readings as the law is interwoven into our everyday lives, ranging from work or employment contracts, rental agreements, house sale contracts, wills and inheritances, to litigation, situations involving the police, or courts of law. If someone asks a question relating to any of these types of situations, Justice is one of the cards you would anticipate being present and, if accompanied by positive cards, can favourably indicate and confirm the associated contract.

Due to the legal implications, there are lots of possible combinations. Always check the defined meanings you normally use and follow progressions carefully to avoid misinterpretation or jumping to conclusions. I would normally look for a number of reinforcing cards when less favourable indications are present, although this is more evident when using larger spreads, such as the Life Spread and Anchor.

In direct questions concerning litigation or court appearances, you would hope to find a favourable card immediately following Justice to show a good out-come and happy resolution. When serious legal matters are a cause for concern or form part of the question, it can be equally telling should the card be absent, which often indicates matters being settled out of court or charges being dropped.

On a personal level, the message from Justice advises the need for a logical mind and balanced thought, time to weigh all the facts involved, and to come to a decision that is honest and fair to everyone concerned.

Reversed or Badly Aspected

Complications in a legal matter, injustices, being unfairly dealt with or impli-cated, a ruling not in your favour, miscarriage of justice, or sometimes corrup-tion (although normally in association with other cards in that instance).

Associations

Similar and Supporting Cards: Ace of Pentacles (material contracts), the Emperor (rational thought), the Hermit (contemplation), Temperance (balanced emotions), King or Queen of Swords (lawyers, police—people with a legal connection), Two of Pentacles (maintaining balance).

Opposing and Contradictory Cards: Five of Wands (out of balance), **Two of Swords** (indecision, two minds), **Five of Swords** (dishonourable), **the Devil** (corruption).

Justice Featured Combinations

Two of Wands > Justice: Legal documents can be indicated in relation to a working partnership, for instance a formal agreement. Be fair-minded and take a balanced approach with working partners and groups.

Three of Wands > Justice: A commercial lease or business contract. Progress or expansion leads to legal matters, contracts, or agreements coming into play.

Five of Wands > Justice > Temperance: Can be mediation and dispute resolution. This combination highlights the need for a completely balanced approach, both in thought and emotion, but progressively improves towards a successful compromise.

Justice > Seven of Wands > the Sun: Challenging a legal situation and winning.

Justice > Page of Swords > Knight of Wands: Minor delays with legal matters but the house move will proceed in due course.

Justice > Ten of Swords: A disappointing ending to a legal matter; unfortunately, as things stand, this is not lining up to go in your favour. Can be a legal contract rescinded.

Ace of Pentacles > the Hierophant > the Emperor > Justice: Important documentation connected to higher authorities. I've seen this combination in relation to applying to the relevant government ministry for a foreign visa, also for court applications in higher matters. Due to the Ace of Pentacles at the beginning it normally involves the submission and application, the start of the process, that requires permission from authorities to proceed.

Eight of Pentacles > Justice: New work contract or agreement, contract of employment (can appear in opposite order too).

Justice > Nine of Pentacles: A lucrative contract, or a substantial legal payment being made to you.

Ten of Pentacles > Three of Swords > Justice: Family dispute leads to legal action. Can also suggest a dispute concerning a property matter, but check the preceding card to see where it originates from or whom with.

The Hierophant > Justice > Ten of Cups: Exchanging vows, marriage, and official documents such as a marriage certificate; can sometimes show **Ace of Pentacles** instead of Justice for the certificate (other marriage cards would normally also be evident in the spread).

The Moon > Justice > the Devil: Suggests a cover-up and the potential for an injustice, corruption. The Moon and the Devil can also follow Justice. Similar interpretation when appearing with the Five of Swords instead of the Moon.

Collectively, watch for: The Emperor, the Hierophant, and Justice together indicate a situation dealing with higher authorities, government, law of the land, etc.

XII–The Hanged Man

Major Arcana (Trumps or Triumphs): Symbolic life experiences. Worldly affairs.

Flow: None; motionless

Polarity: Neutral

Multiple Majors: Milestones and significant life events. Catalyst.

Keywords and Phrases: Suspension, limbo. Reassessment.

Applied Meaning

When the Hanged Man appears in a reading, it often shows that something is going to slow down and come to a grinding halt, so nothing will be going anywhere at that stage. For this reason, it can be one of the most frustrating cards in the deck, as most people want to forge ahead with their plans, not see them held up in any way.

Wherever this card appears, you can anticipate a delaying effect that can sometimes be quite lengthy. However, there is usually a good reason, so it provides the opportunity for reassessment. As the Hanged Man is upside down, he sees life through a different lens and altered perception. It may be time to get creative and think outside the box or engage in some lateral thinking to see things from a completely fresh and different perspective.

Sometimes we can become quite fixated on one particular pathway, but when nothing is happening or if things become stuck or aren't gaining traction, it can encourage us to take the blinkers off and see things from every other possible angle. A fresh perspective could lead to a new insight to find a solution and move things forwards.

There are occasions when it may feel as though circumstances are outside of your control with other factors affecting the situation, such that you feel as if you are dangling in midair. Sometimes we need to exercise patience or wait for all the interconnecting pieces to slot into place, which may not always be evident or at the convenience of our own timetable.

The element of sacrifice can be topical with this card, although it is usually a small sacrifice in the short term to gain something of greater value in the longer term—sometimes you need to lose the battle to win the war. Due to some past historical connections to the card, some people see the meaning as a traitor and this may be so when badly aspected in the right combination.

Reversed or Badly Aspected

Inability to see outside of a fixed or possibly biased perspective. Victimhood. An informant, traitor, treachery, and betrayal.

Associations

Similar and Supporting Cards: Two of Swords (stalemate, non-movement) is the main accompanying and supportive card. Others that can suggest the inactive aspect: **Four of Swords** (withdrawal), **Four of Pentacles** (pull back), and **Eight of Swords** (restriction). To some extent, the unconventional aspect of **the Fool**, when looking at reassessment. All slow-moving or delaying cards would emphasise this facet: **Page of Swords** (delays), **Knight of Pentacles**, and **the Hermit** (contemplation but also very slow).

Opposing and Contradictory Cards: The Hierophant (conventional), **Two of Pentacles** (flowing). All fast-moving and action cards when looking at this aspect, such as: **the Chariot, Eight of Wands, Knight of Swords**.

The Hanged Man Featured Combinations

Ace of Wands > the Hanged Man: Immediate slowdown; a new project is suspended; original plans will need to be reviewed and reassessed.

Two of Wands > the Hanged Man: Timeframes extended to initial plans; frozen deadlines; prepare contingency measures in advance. Joint venture may need re-evaluation.

Knight of Wands > the Hanged Man: Significant delays with a planned house move (can also appear in opposite order).

Ace of Cups > Eight of Wands > the Hanged Man > Five of Cups: For singles, can be a sign of ghosting, wherein a new relationship gets off to a quick start but then there is no response to communications, and upset follows.

Two of Cups > the Hanged Man > Four of Cups: A relationship may plateau or feel stalled and not developing; a relationship becoming stale leaves you jaded and dissatisfied.

Three of Cups > the Hanged Man: Can represent the postponement of an upcoming social event.

Two of Swords > Wheel of Fortune > the Hanged Man: Trapped in a loop and going round in a circle; inability to realise opportunities, reassessment needed. Also ...

Two of Swords > Judgement > the Hanged Man: ... can also show a repeating cycle in which things aren't going anywhere.

Four of Swords > the Hanged Man: Usually indicates a fallow period; also applies in the opposite order but in a more restorative fashion.

Page of Swords > the Hanged Man > the Devil: Takes a more negative form with the potential for an informant or traitor. The **Five of Swords** could also feature.

Three of Pentacles > the Hanged Man: Unable to move a work matter ahead due to delays that could take some time. For some, can represent a glass-ceiling situation in a work position—check other indications in the spread.

The Chariot > the Hanged Man: Unstoppable force meets an immovable object! Something is hurtling towards a brick wall; slow down and reassess. Whereas ...

The Hanged Man > the Chariot: ... would show release from the situation in question; charging out the gate and full steam ahead after lengthy delays.

The Hermit > the Hanged Man > the Fool: Can point to radical and innovative thinking to break through barriers. (The Hermit and the Hanged Man may also appear in the opposite order.)

XIII–Death

Major Arcana (Trumps or Triumphs): Symbolic life experiences. Worldly affairs.

Flow: Stop

Polarity: Negative

Multiple Majors: Milestones and significant life events. Catalyst.

Keywords and Phrases: Ending. Major change and transformation.

Applied Meaning

Death is perhaps one of the easiest cards to work with in combinations, for whatever it follows shows that it will be coming to an end. This is the card of closure and where something has reached the end of its natural cycle. Death brings down the final curtain and, unless followed by Judgement to resurrect matters, brings events to their natural conclusion in a definite ending.

This is one of the external cards in that the situation is usually outside the client's control. Wherever this ending appears, it brings release but also a major change—an area of life will be transformed as a result. Whilst people often try to resist or fear change, not all endings are negative and it can be helpful if someone is transitioning from one phase of life into another—the ending of a difficult divorce or a particularly stressful situation, for instance. Equally, you may find it presents itself for someone undergoing a major change in their life with positive circumstances which, as always, will be reflected in the surrounding cards.

On a personal level, the cleansing influence of Death can be used in a beneficial way that helps release things that no longer serve you, such as bad habits or toxic baggage. Finally, you may find this card around someone if they are experiencing the grieving process, if there has been a loss in their life of something important to them, or in connection with legacies—not usually the prediction of an actual, physical death.

Reversed or Badly Aspected

A prolonged ending, stagnation, refusal or resistance to change that only serves to extend matters. An inability to move on.

Associations

Similar and Supporting Cards: Ten of Swords (ending), **Wheel of Fortune** (change) and **multiple Sevens** indicate a cycle change; **multiple Tens** show a period of completion.

Opposing and Contradictory Cards: The **Aces** and **the Fool**, indicating new beginnings.

Death Featured Combinations

Ace of Wands > Death: A flash in the pan; a new start comes to a swift close; something that's over almost as soon as it has begun. If another positive card follows, it can then denote a whole new way of life that brings complete change and a transformation of lifestyle.

Death > Knight of Wands: Major change and a house move (can be emigration), whereas…

Knight of Wands > Death: …a cancelled house move.

Death > Five of Cups > Six of Pentacles: Can represent a bereavement, mourning, and inheritance (if the **Five** and **Six** are in the opposite order, you may be disappointed). The Ten of Pentacles can also feature, but mainly for a family legacy, as below…

Death > Ten of Pentacles: Family inheritance matters, can also include: **Justice**, **Six of Pentacles**, and **Ace of Pentacles** in combination or immediate surrounding cards.

Eight of Cups > Death: This would usually indicate the client's decision to walk away and bring something to an end (check preceding card, if available, to see what this would be. In the Life Spread, the title of the area would usually pinpoint it for you).

Ten of Cups > Death: Can indicate a marriage annulment or the end of a committed relationship. Also…

The Lovers > Death: …the end of the affair, a romantic relationship ending.

Ace of Pentacles > Death: Can be the termination of a contract, would be unlikely to proceed. Whereas…

Death > Justice > Ace of Pentacles: …can indicate a last will and testament.

Knight of Pentacles > Three of Swords > Death: A long-standing dispute finally comes to a close.

Death > Wheel of Fortune > the Fool: Complete and absolute change from one path to another that is usually fortunate; out with the old and in with the new.

Death > Judgement: Something that ended is resurrected (check the spread area or the card preceding Death to identify it).

XIV–Temperance

Major Arcana (Trumps or Triumphs): Symbolic life experiences. Worldly affairs.

Flow: Gently flowing

Polarity: Positive

Multiple Majors: Milestones and significant life events. Catalyst.

Keywords and Phrases: Patience. Moderation. Harmonious balance. Renewal and healing.

Applied Meaning

Temperance is the card of harmony and balance, so it suggests taking a moderate approach in matters and being tolerant, calm, and diplomatic in all your dealings. It may be necessary to take the middle path and exercise patience both with people and situations.

Patience can be easier in theory than in practice but, just as the alchemist carefully blends and integrates the opposing elements, it leads to a successful conclusion that serves a greater good. Compromise may be necessary to attain a spirit of cooperation and achieve a satisfactory outcome that is mutually beneficial, but the gentle touch of Temperance indicates it can be done.

In all types of relationships, this card provides the required recipe for healing and renewal—olive branches can be proffered, ruffled feathers smoothed, and bridges mended; it is a particularly good sign for resolving differences when following the Three of Swords, Five of Cups, or any disruptive influences you may find. The healing aspect of the Temperance card can also feature in combinations connected to physical health and well-being.

Temperance is the card of emotional balance, so it is not unusual to find it appear in situations for those in a long-standing and harmonious relationship, and sometimes alongside the Two of Cups to reinforce the deep and compatible shared bond.

Reversed or Badly Aspected

Out of balance, lack of cooperation, impatience and intolerance, lack of self-restraint.

Associations

> **Similar and Supporting Cards: The Star** (healing), **Judgement** (renewal), **Two of Cups** (harmonious bond), **Six of Cups** (past aspect connects with renewal), **Two of Pentacles** (maintaining balance), **Strength** (diplomacy); **Justice** is complementary, the balanced mind to the balanced emotions of Temperance. Slower-moving cards would reinforce the care and patience aspect, such as **the Hermit**, etc.
>
> **Opposing and Contradictory Cards: The Devil** (excess), **Five of Wands** (friction), **Three of Swords** (stormy emotions), **Five of Swords** (hostile), **the Chariot** and **the Emperor** (forceful energy).

Temperance Featured Combinations

Two of Wands > Temperance: The art of diplomacy in dealing with others, compromise in working relationships; patience will be required as you move forwardss.

Temperance > Two of Cups: Always a lovely combination for relationships that shows things are well-balanced and harmonious and that the couple are perfectly attuned; bodes well for the future. Can also appear in the opposite order.

Three of Swords > Temperance: Patience and diplomacy can help resolve differences and defuse simmering tensions towards finding compromise.

Temperance > Four of Swords > the Star: A period of rest and convalescence may be necessary, an improvement to health and general well-being; note how the two healing cards sandwich the card of rest and recovery to reinforce the meaning. (Also see **Four of Swords**, page 119 and **the Hierophant**, page 217 for hospitals.)

Three of Pentacles > Two of Pentacles > Temperance: Indicates multitasking at work, wearing many hats or juggling more than one job or project; you have the ability to pull things off and keep the flow going whilst retaining a sense of balance in the process.

Temperance > Knight of Pentacles: Biding your time will bring dividends, and matters will come to fruition, although it could take a while; patience will be needed but provides the opportunity to carefully sift through and take care of all the details.

The Chariot > Temperance: Moderating your approach, reining things in and showing some restraint would prove to be a better policy as you move forwards.

The Lovers > Five of Cups > Temperance: Would show a temporary upset but healing and renewal following, found through compromise. **Judgement** instead of Temperance would also show reconciliation.

Temperance > the Hermit: Take your time and carefully think things through; re-emphasises patience.

Justice > Temperance: Can show legal mediation or conciliation for dispute resolution (particularly if preceded by the **Three of Swords** or **Five of Wands**.) In personal matters, this combination highlights the need for a balanced mind and emotions (head and heart). In the opposite order...

Temperance > Justice: ... in legal matters, it can show arbitration.

The Devil > Temperance: May suggest self-restraint and moderating excessive behaviour or destructive habits in order to overcome and be healed from them.

Collectively, watch for cards connected to healing appearing together in combinations: Temperance and the Star (healing), Four of Swords (convalescence), Six of Swords (recovery), the Hierophant (hospital), the Eight of Swords (confinement).

XV–THE DEVIL

Major Arcana (Trumps or Triumphs): Symbolic life experiences. Worldly affairs.

Flow: Blocked

Polarity: Negative

Multiple Majors: Milestones and significant life events. Catalyst.

Keywords and Phrases: Unhealthy behaviour. Shadow side. Secret plans.

Applied Meaning

Although most cards can have a shadow side, the Devil *is* the shadow side: it can highlight and amplify the darker elements of human nature. Wherever the Devil appears, it tends to tarnish and corrupt the card it follows, as though leading it astray, bringing out the negative aspects and making it tainted and toxic. In a simple line, we would hope to find it followed by a positive card to bring release or neutralise the effect moving forwards.

Whilst Temperance recommends self-restraint and moderation, the Devil can show excessive behaviour or something out of control where restraint is sorely lacking. Hedonistic tendencies or overindulgence can lead to unhealthy habits such as addictions of all description, whether alcohol or substance abuse, gambling, overspending, or sexual behaviour. Whatever the Devil card follows usually becomes excessive, extreme, or oppressive in some way.

In relationships (and with the right combinations), it can suggest obsession, controlling or manipulative behaviour, a clandestine affair, or abuse of some description—check surrounding cards carefully for verification. Every card falls somewhere within a spectrum and, unlike the Devil, we don't have to rush straight to the extremes immediately and think the worst. That said, this card does usually point to something unhealthy.

The oppressive energy of the card can show the client is feeling completely bogged down, enslaved, and consumed by a situation they feel unable to release themselves from; you will be able to recognise when something weighs heavily upon them.

In combinations, watch for the Devil and Five of Swords sandwiching or surrounding other cards, as it can point to murky or nefarious activities, depending upon other cards, of course. In a similar situation with the Moon or Seven of Swords, it can show matters being cloaked and hidden and, collectively, they can point to a bagful of trouble you would probably prefer to avoid. Again, always look for backup from other cards. You will find various combinations involving these cards scattered throughout the book, as they frequently hang around together—a surefire way of recognising something is amiss.

The Devil can also show aspects of secrecy ranging from dubious behaviour to keeping your cards close to your chest for good reason, such as an invention or new product release, for instance. It can also refer to something that you may not wish to be in the public domain for the moment. Sometimes (but usually quite rarely) it can suggest an improvement in your sex life.

Reversed or Badly Aspected

The Devil reversed is often a complete reversal, so it can show release from an addictive or oppressive situation. When badly aspected or surrounded by negative cards (upright), it tends to accentuate the negative side.

Associations

Similar and Supporting Cards: **Ten of Wands** (burdens), **Eight of Swords** (restriction), **Nine of Swords** (anxiety). All the secrecy cards appearing anywhere across a larger spread would also highlight this aspect. **Five of Swords** (dubious activities), **the Moon** (deception), **the High Priestess** would reinforce the overlap and underlying message of secrecy as part of a group, although individually from a favourable angle, as the secret being revealed. **Seven of Swords** (stealth).

Opposing and Contradictory Cards: **Temperance** (moderation), **the Star** (hope and optimism), **the Hierophant** (morals and ethics). All success and triumph cards that also can help to lessen or override the negative effects.

The Devil Featured Combinations

Ace of Wands > the Devil: Watch your step: you may feel trapped by whatever is being started. New plans could weigh you down, making you enslaved to a new business or project, or discovering a new job has a toxic work environment. Whereas...

The Devil > Ace of Wands (or **Eight of Pentacles**): ... keeping your cards close to your chest regarding starting a new venture; a secret plan is about to be hatched—the progression of the cards shows this should come to pass.

Three of Wands > the Devil: You may not feel ready to launch your ships or you're keeping future activities under wraps for the moment. You could be feeling bogged down with what initial success has brought into play; possibly working too hard based on earlier success, the unintended consequences of being a victim of your own success.

Seven of Swords > Five of Swords > the Devil: Underworld, gangland, criminal activities, and organised crime. **The Moon** may feature, for veiled activities.

The Magician > the Devil: A con artist; trickery, manipulation.

The Emperor > the Devil: Power corrupts … The bullying or tyrannical boss, power-hungry or egotistical leader. Alternatively, a leadership position drags you down.

The Devil > Temperance: The perfect antidote, balancing out the extremes and moderating behaviour towards healing and recovery.

Some of the Excesses of Life …

Three of Pentacles > the Devil: Workaholic tendencies.

Four of Pentacles > the Devil: Hoarding, being miserly.

Five of Pentacles > the Devil: Compulsive overspending, shopaholic, excessive debt.

Three of Cups > the Devil: A party animal; a wild night out; maybe too much of a good thing. Toxic friends.

Six of Cups > the Devil: Unable to let go of the past, possible obsession with an old flame.

Nine of Cups > the Devil: Can be overindulgence with food and drink, but also a warning to be careful what you wish for—it will cause you problems later.

The Lovers > the Devil: Could be an intoxicating but unhealthy attraction; great sex but not good for a long-term future; a one-night stand; fetishes; addictions; possibly abuse, or a toxic relationship.

Wheel of Fortune > the Devil: Gambling addiction.

> *If the Devil is followed by **the Star, the Sun, Four of Swords,** or **Six of Swords,** it would show recovery from a difficult situation—most of the positive cards following would show release.*

XVI–The Tower

Major Arcana (Trumps or Triumphs): Symbolic life experiences. Worldly affairs.

Flow: Abrupt jolt

Polarity: Negative

Multiple Majors: Milestones and significant life events.

Keywords and Phrases: Disruption. Unexpected upheaval.

Applied Meaning

The Tower brings sudden and unexpected upheaval, so it tends to indicate unanticipated events with a disruptive influence. Shocks and surprises of the less favourable variety are usually suggested but, just as with all the cards, it operates across a full range of possibilities. It is probably the card we least hope to see in our reading; the common automatic reaction is to immediately fear the absolute worst.

Although the Tower is an unwelcome guest wherever it lands, it operates in degrees ranging from an incident that rattles your cage and leaves you fizzing to a catastrophe that shakes everything up, the demolishment of something you believed to be a carefully constructed part of your universe. The common denominator that binds these differing events is usually the shock factor or the unexpected nature that brings it to your door. Although it can be challenging, the Tower can bring a raw flash of insight that allows you to see beyond the clutter it clears away, allowing you to build anew from a stronger foundation.

In larger spreads, it can be easier to see to what extent the client's life will be affected. If the Tower looks out of place and is unsupported by similar and negative cards, it can represent an isolated incident that will have minimal impact upon different areas of life other than where it appears; surrounding cards should inform you as to the nature of the event.

Conversely, the type of extreme situation we most fear has a ricochet effect and the impact can clearly be seen right across the spread, which is usually negatively aspected throughout. This is quite rare, so most Tower situations you come across should be to a much lesser degree. Everyone will encounter a myriad of differing Tower experiences throughout the course of their life, so surrounding cards should help to keep things in perspective

In combinations, this is an easy card to work with, as the card it follows shows where the sudden change comes from or what may collapse as a result. When it appears in future positions, it can provide the opportunity to consider alternative plans.

Reversed or Badly Aspected

Usually similar in meaning but to a lesser degree; some see it as a suggestion of danger averted.

Associations

Similar and Supporting Cards: Ten of Swords (disappointing ending), **Death** (finality and closure).

Opposing and Contradictory: Nine of Cups (wish card), **the Sun** (happiness), and most of the positive cards. **The Star** and **Temperance** (calm and healing).

The Tower Featured Combinations

Seven of Wands > the Tower: Something could shake your core beliefs. Taking a strong stance and pursuing the matter could backfire, so step down for the moment and don't issue any ultimatums.

Eight of Wands > the Tower: News of a shocking nature that causes upheaval and shakes things up.

The Tower > Eight of Cups: You may feel there's nothing further to be salvaged from this situation and the best course of action would be to walk away and direct your energy elsewhere. Cutting your losses.

Three of Swords > the Tower: An explosive row. Bickering or a squabble that blows up and escalates out of proportion to the initial disagreement—handle with care.

Three of Pentacles > the Tower > Five of Pentacles: Can indicate surprise and sudden loss connected to your main work, such as an unexpected redundancy, a client who fails to pay and leaves you in a difficult position, or a sudden cancellation of work you weren't anticipating that will result in a hit to finances. The Five is usually temporary, though, so look for improving conditions further into the spread. Whereas ...

Nine of Pentacles > the Tower: ... could show more substantial disruption to financial position.

The Fool > the Tower: Spontaneous combustion! The Fool is badly aspected here, so it can suggest foolhardy action—walking straight into trouble.

The High Priestess > the Tower: Bombshell revelations; information released causes a major disruption. If followed by ...

The High Priestess > the Tower > the Moon: ... the information that comes to light that caused the upset can't be trusted. Note how the Tower is now surrounded by two secrecy cards: The High Priestess can't progress positively as it is followed by two negative cards, and The Moon is influenced by the negative aspect. Taken together, they introduce the murky side of smoke and mirrors and possible deceptions.

The Tower > Wheel of Fortune: This is the order we would prefer to find this pairing, as it shows a positive uplift after facing challenges and good luck about to turn in your favour.

The Devil > the Tower: This can be a dangerous or violent combination that is best avoided, so would recommend the client extricate themselves if showing in future positions. If you have an additional preceding card, or sometimes central between these two, it can highlight the area of concern. Sometimes it can indicate abuse, but there will normally be further indications in the spread.

The Emperor > the Tower: For those who read global trends and events, it can be an indication of conflict or war; **the Devil** may also be present.

The World > the Tower: Thankfully, this combination very rarely makes an appearance. Two of the biggest cards in the deck that are completely opposite to each other, The Tower brings a shock disruption and possibly destruction, quite a spectacular "fall from grace" from the pinnacle of success.

XVII–The Star

Major Arcana (Trumps or Triumphs): Symbolic life experiences. Worldly affairs.

Flow: Gently flowing

Polarity: Positive

Multiple Majors: Milestones and significant life events. Catalyst.

Keywords and Phrases: Hope. Healing. Improvement. Inspiration.

Applied Meaning

The Star will always bring a smile to your reading, as it suggests hope and optimism for the future. Wherever it lands, you can be assured that brighter times are on the horizon and conditions will improve. As a natural progression in the order of the majors, it seems fitting that the message of hope and healing should follow the disruptive influences experienced in the Tower.

Wherever you see challenging aspects, the Star is one of the cards you hope to find following it as a sign that uplifting conditions are on the way. The Star is like the gentle hug within the tarot and the ultimate cure-all, although it tends to suggest improving circumstances that gradually unfold rather than as an immediate effect, unless found in a present position in the spread.

The gentle light of the Star can act as a soothing healing balm to a difficult situation, whether to a rift or health and well-being. For those who may have experienced hurt, it encourages belief in the future, assured in its promise that brighter prospects are destined. It's time to pick up the baton again and turn your attention to better days yet to come.

When appearing alongside a new relationship or marriage cards, it adds blessings and the prospect of a promising future. In career matters, it can show inspired thought but is also an excellent card for anyone working in the public eye and, with the right cards, may suggest the time has come to shine. Find your due north and follow your star.

Reversed or Badly Aspected

Feeling discouraged, lacking hope and losing faith in the future.

Associations

Similar and Supporting Cards: Temperance (healing), **Six of Swords** (calm after storm), **Six of Wands** (acclaim).

Opposing and Contradictory Cards: Ten of Wands or **the Devil** (weighed down), **Four of Cups** (uninspired), **Nine of Swords** (anxiety), **the Tower** (disruption).

The Star Featured Combinations

Ace of Wands > the Star: Creative and inspired thought for a new project. Brings blessings to new ventures and bodes well for the future.

Three of Wands > the Star: Hopeful influences keep you on track, earlier gains bring inspiration, overall improvement on its way. Progress and expansion in commercial endeavours are well-aspected.

Six of Wands > the Chariot > the Star: Victory parade; this combination brings accolades, honours, and acclaim with public recognition.

Ace of Cups > the Star: Sealed with a gentle kiss! For singles, a new relationship holds a promising future. For those attached, a new beginning for the family holds happiness and blessings for the future.

The Star > Four of Cups: Despite the appearance of promising conditions, things may not live up to your expectations and leave you flat or uninspired. Ensure that you are fully investigating the potential within this situation, as you could miss the promise it holds.

Knight of Cups > the Star: This offer or proposal is worthy of investigation as it portends a bright future where you can do well and improve your overall situation. A preceding card would help to identify the nature of the offer.

Four of Swords > the Star: A period of convalescence, recovery, and healing. Temperance would be similar to the Star, and if the Hierophant is included, it may suggest a hospital stay (see the Hierophant combinations, page 217).

Nine of Swords > the Star: The ideal combination we like to see—from worrying concerns to matters improving; bringing hope and optimism for the future.

Ten of Swords > the Star: The ending of a difficult situation allows for healing to begin and life will start to turn the corner; brighter days are on the horizon.

The Star > Four of Pentacles: Be careful you're not holding yourself back or being overly cautious concerning something where conditions look bright and encouraging.

The Star > the Hermit > the Magician: Putting inspired thought into action and mastering your talents (a good combination for writers and those in communication fields).

The Sun > the Star > the World: Hitting the big time—it's your time to shine! With the Star placed central, it would place you in the spotlight, but these three together in any order indicate success on a grander scale than usual. Particularly relevant for those who work in the entertainment industry or in the public eye. Fame.

XVIII–THE MOON

Major Arcana (Trumps or Triumphs): Symbolic life experiences. Worldly affairs.

Flow: Still

Polarity: Negative

Multiple Majors: Milestones and significant life events. Catalyst.

Keywords and Phrases: Uncertainty. Unknown factors. Secrecy. Illusion.

Applied Meaning

The Moon surrounds events with an element of mystery and can indicate a period of uncertainty due to unknown factors. Emotions may fluctuate from one extreme to another whilst leaving a sense of being all at sea, where nothing appears to be quite as it seems. The Moon invades your sense of stability, creates shapes in the shadows and illusionary situations, and provokes your worst fears to surface.

Shifting circumstances can throw you off-balance, and it may feel as though you are wading through fog. Information and answers seem to be veiled in a cloak of shadows, so it can be hard to find clarity and get your bearings or know where you stand in a situation, leaving you questioning whether you can trust your instincts or if you may be imagining things.

I find there is usually a second act with the Moon—something always follows and, as it can suggest clouded thinking, what you see initially is often not the full picture. The best advice is not to jump to conclusions but wait until all the facts are available, as they will rise to the surface in the fullness of time.

There can be aspects of smoke and mirrors in a situation: most particularly, when accompanied by the other secrecy cards and badly aspected with negative cards, it can suggest deceptions, although to a lesser degree it can point to half-truths that muddy the waters and create confusion. With the right combinations, it can show things hidden or veiled activity, so surface or outward appearances can be deceptive.

The Moon can be favourable for heightened awareness, dreams, intuition, and psychic ability, suggesting it may be time to listen to your instincts, but as mentioned above, careful judgement is recommended—be aware but watch and wait.

Reversed or Badly Aspected

Deception, delusion, paranoia, suspicion, false friends, hidden enemies, insincerity, a receding or waning situation, something on the way out.

Associations

Similar and Supporting Cards: **Seven of Cups** (can cloud realistic thinking), **Two of Swords** (indecision), **Nine of Swords** (anxiety). Watch for: **The Devil**, **Five of Swords**, and **the High Priestess** to reinforce aspects of secrecy. **Seven of Swords** (stealth). When the Moon appears with multiple **Fives**, it accentuates the message of instability.

Opposing and Contradictory Cards: **The Emperor** (stability, logic, and rationale), **Justice** (balanced mind), **Ace of Swords** (clarity), **Temperance** (balanced emotions).

The Moon Featured Combinations

Two of Wands > the Moon: Wavering and the inability to see ahead clearly; lingering doubts as to how to move forwards; concern over a working partner and uncertainty with trust.

Eight of Wands > the Moon: News comes in quickly, but don't take things at face value—you don't have all the information yet and some elements may be concealed. Whereas...

The Moon > Eight Wands: ... in the opposite order, it may signal information coming through to release the uncertainty of matters.

Knight of Cups > the Moon > Four of Cups: Take your time to investigate this offer further because something is amiss and would not live up to your expectations or leave you dissatisfied; there are undisclosed factors at play.

Nine of Cups > the Moon > Ace of Swords: Waiting for the other shoe to drop. When the Moon is surrounded by positive cards, it can show triggered anxiety or anticipating the worst in a good situation where it is unfounded. As a progression, the Ace of Swords clears the cobwebs to bring strength and clarity on a new path; overcoming the mental monsters.

The Moon > Five of Swords: The reinforcement of these two cards in this order points to deliberate deception for personal gain; someone around you can't be trusted.

Eight of Swords > the Moon > Nine of Swords: Worries and anxiety may be getting out of hand, creating turmoil and despair. Fears can be verging on paranoia, particularly if the cards seem isolated without any underlying reason being apparent in the other surrounding cards.

Five of Pentacles > the Moon: Financial insecurity; a material loss leads to an uncertain outlook and clouded thinking. Ideally, we wish to see a positive card following to show release and resolution to the problem.

Any King of Queen > the Moon: The court card would provide a good description of the person involved but the Moon following surrounds them with mystery. It doesn't necessarily represent someone who can't be trusted but may suggest a lot more depth and information they may not be disclosing—proceed cautiously.

The Chariot > the Moon: Metaphorically driving through fog—guard against confidence overriding logic and take time to plan before surging forwards, as it suggests hurtling into uncertainty; all is not as it seems and you could become unstuck.

The Moon > the Devil: Trippy! In relation to addictions, it can suggest substance abuse, hallucinations, or delusional and unstable behaviour.

The Magician > the Devil > the Moon: Can show manipulation and/or gaslighting that could leave you feeling confused and second-guessing yourself—do not believe what you are being told, as the truth is being twisted and concealed.

Collectively, watch for all the secrecy cards appearing anywhere on the table in a larger spread, as it reveals underlying secrecy surrounding the client: Five of Swords, Seven of Swords, the High Priestess, the Devil, the Moon.

XIX–THE SUN

Major Arcana (Trumps or Triumphs): Symbolic life experiences. Worldly affairs.

Flow: Steady

Polarity: Positive

Multiple Majors: Milestones and significant life events. Catalyst.

Keywords and Phrases: Happiness. Success. Vitality.

Applied Meaning

The Sun is one of the most positive cards in the deck; it brightens any scene and brings good cheer to all situations. Everything is uplifted in the presence of the Sun—enterprises flourish, relationships bring happiness, health matters improve and vitality is restored, and your projects and endeavours see shining success.

This is an excellent card for success and achievement that, although not quite as potent as the World, still adds a significant boost in combinations. One of the strengths of this card is the way it can intensify other favourable cards around it, just as all living things reach and respond to the light and warmth of our sun. All is well in the world wherever the sun shines and its radiance blesses our lives with happiness and joyful contentment.

In a simple line formation, the Sun can turn almost any situation into a positive when it trumps as the last card. Whilst its appearance can invigorate even the darkest corners, we prefer to find it following a negative card to show an uplift and positive resolution to the matter. Watch for situations where the Sun is sandwiched between negative cards: although there may be brief respite, it would still be hampered by the card that follows in the progression of events and have difficulty manifesting the good vibes. In positional spreads, the placement title would be the guiding principle.

Similarly, the Sun provides an additional boost to amplify financial affairs when it appears alongside cards of a material nature, suggesting you will be more than happy with the outcome, rather than the card indicating prosperity in its own right. Finally and on a more mundane level, it can suggest sunnier climes, most particularly when appearing with travel cards.

Reversed or Badly Aspected

The Sun is one of the few cards that remains relatively unchanged when reversed; outcomes are similar, only to a lesser degree. When badly aspected, it can prevent the Sun from attaining its highest potential. Although an extremely positive card, it cannot override a negative card following, when read in a straight line progression.

Associations

Similar and Supporting Cards: Nine of Cups (wish card), **the World** (success and achievement), **Three of Cups** (celebration). All positive cards would relate and strengthen it.

Opposing and Contradictory Cards: The Tower (collapse and disruption), **Nine of Swords** (worry and anxiety), **Four of Cups** (discontent), **Five of Cups** (sadness). All negative cards.

The Sun Featured Combinations

Eight of Wands > the Sun > Six of Swords: Here the travel aspect is emphasised: the Sun is sandwiched between two travel cards to reinforce a journey to sunny climes.

Ten of Wands > the Sun > Four of Pentacles: Once bitten, twice shy; the Sun shows release from an overwhelming situation that results in overcaution moving forwards, perhaps for good reason.

Eight of Cups > the Sun: Making the right call; abandoning a path that has drained you will prove to be the right decision and should work out better than you imagine.

Ten of Cups > Ten of Pentacles > the Sun: Abundant blessings in home and family life; emotional and material contentment.

Two of Swords > the Moon > the Sun: As different as night and day, a situation that has been mired with indecision and lack of clarity becomes illuminated, allowing you to make excellent progress as you move forwards.

Four of Swords > the Sun: Rest and recovery brings a return to vitality and improvement to well-being.

Nine of Swords > the Sun > Ten of Swords: Although the Sun provides a brief reprieve, worst fears may eventually be realised, bringing a disappointing ending. Surrounded in this way, it shows the Sun is unable to fully manifest its potential, but the Ten of Swords is far enough in the timeline that alternative action could be taken now in an effort to avert the situation lining up.

Eight of Pentacles > the Sun: New work that fulfils you and holds a bright future.

Justice > Knight of Pentacles > Ace of Swords > the Sun: Can represent winning a legal case to your complete satisfaction after lengthy proceedings.

The Sun > the Tower: Short-lived happiness or success (similarly, Death or Ten of Swords), whereas …

The Tower > the Sun: … can show something that initially appears to be a disaster turns out surprisingly well and for the best.

The World > the Sun: Amplifies accomplishment; can thus indicate a high level of success and usually an event outside of normal circumstances or usual experience. Watch for these two following or sandwiching another card, which could also help to provide more information.

XX–JUDGEMENT

Major Arcana (Trumps or Triumphs): Symbolic life experiences. Worldly affairs.

Flow: Steady

Polarity: Positive

Multiple Majors: Milestones and significant life events.

Keywords and Phrases: Resurrection, revival, renewal. Reconciliation.

Applied Meaning

The implication of Judgment Day is not so much the act of being judged rather than a reawakening based on karmic action; a review of past matters that may have led to this point with the ability to find truth and clarity within it, so to be liberated and born anew. An old situation can present itself where a past lesson can be learnt and the slate wiped clean, allowing release and renewal with a fresh start.

Judgement often represents a revisit of some description and I often think of it as the do-over, second time around, or Lazarus card, for it resurrects something and brings it back to life in order to be re-evaluated. It provides a unique opportunity to assess past aspects and can breathe new life into something that may have lain dormant. Wherever you find this card it suggests there is some history and background and, while it may lead to a new path, it is borne out of an old one. To discover what is being resurrected, check the surrounding cards.

In readings, we are frequently asked about past relationships; Judgement is the main card I would look for to indicate the potential for reconciliation. There are generally three main cards present in these circumstances: the Six of Cups brings someone from the past back onto the radar, Temperance can bring renewal, but Judgement resurrects and reconciles. The three cards often all appear in the reading and act as a strong indicator and reinforcement. For some, it can indicate a revival in your love life following inactivity, but it often points to an old relationship being reborn.

Judgement is the one card that can revive and reopen a door following the Death card, which otherwise contains an element of finality.

Reversed or Badly Aspected

Caught in a holding pattern through refusal to deal with past aspects; denial or rejection through doubt or fears; hesitancy in accepting new circumstances to move on.

Associations

> **Similar and Supporting Cards: Six of Cups** (past aspects), **Temperance** (renewal).
>
> **Opposing and Contradictory Cards: The Fool** (new and unknown), the **Aces** (new beginnings), **Death** (ending).

Judgement Featured Combinations

Judgement > Ace of Wands: Breathing new life into an old project; an old idea reimagined. In the opposite order...

Ace of Wands > Judgement: ... although this is new, it will lead to a revival of some description, perhaps by calling upon past connections. Possibly having to restart or redo something over again.

Judgement > Knight of Wands: Revival of a house move.

Two of Cups > Death > Judgement: A clear sign of a reconciled relationship following a previous ending.

Three of Cups > Judgement: Can be an indicator of various types of anniversary celebrations, so check the preceding card to show which. May also appear in the opposite order.

Five of Cups > Judgement > Three of Swords: Resurrecting old hurts can lead to fresh arguments. This combination would also not bode well for reconciliation; although the potential may briefly surface, it still results in going separate ways, usually through disagreement. Watch for a continuing theme of alternating cards moving forwards, such as **Temperance**, as it can show on-off type relationships.

Judgement > Five of Swords: Old dog, old tricks: watch out for a replay of some unscrupulous or dirty dealings; a repeat performance of an earlier scenario.

Judgement > Nine of Swords: Old fears reawakened; if appearing in the opposite order, you have the opportunity to face and learn from them to finally move forwards.

Judgement > Five of Pentacles: The reoccurrence of an old financial problem rears its head and will need to be dealt with. In the opposite order...

Five of Pentacles > Judgement: ... can show paying off old debts and a fresh start with a clean slate.

Ten of Pentacles > Judgement: Can indicate property renovations and home refurbishments.

The Hermit > Eight of Pentacles > Judgement: May indicate studying for resitting exams.

Collectively, watch for: Six of Cups, Temperance, and Judgement appearing together in the same spread, as they reinforce past aspects, renewal, and reconciliation.

XXI–The World

Major Arcana (Trumps or Triumphs): Symbolic life experiences. Worldly affairs.

Flow: Steady

Polarity: Positive

Multiple Majors: Milestones and significant life events.

Keywords and Phrases: Successful completion. Triumphant achievement with joyful rewards.

Applied Meaning

The World brings successful achievement and triumphant attainment with a sense of completion and fulfilment. A common theme of duality can be found throughout the journey of the deck, but in the World all aspects are harmonised and unified into a glorious crowning moment.

The success the World brings is not usually of the overnight variety unless surrounding cards indicate otherwise; more commonly it speaks of something that has been worked towards over a period of time, culminating in a triumphant moment that results in joyful and heartfelt rewards for efforts.

As one of the most positive cards in the deck, the World is the ultimate indicator of success and often has the essence of longevity or at least something longer-term. In whichever area of life this card appears, it suggests that plans reach a successful conclusion and wonderful results are forthcoming, bringing great happiness and fulfilment.

On a more mundane level, the World can indicate international travel or foreign connections.

Reversed and Badly Aspected

Lack of integration, delayed completion, or incomplete plans; sometimes being overambitious, though usually thwarted ambitions through stagnation.

Associations

Similar and Supporting Cards: The World is like a combination of all the positive cards synthesised and woven together within one card: **Nine of Cups** (wish fulfilled), **the Sun** (success and happiness), **the Chariot** (victory over obstacles), **Ace of Swords** (triumph over adversity), **Six of Wands** (acclaim). **Ten of Cups** (emotional happiness), **Ten of Pentacles** (material contentment), **Three of Cups** (celebration), **the Empress** (abundant harvest). All positive cards of success and fulfilment would reinforce those aspects.

Opposing and Contradictory Cards: The **Tower**, **Death**, **Ten of Swords** (unfavourable endings), **the Hanged Man**, **Two of Swords** (stasis), **Five of Cups** (sadness and disappointment), and cards of a negative connotation.

The World Featured Combinations

Ace of Wands > the World: Assured success from the outset. Your new project will be a triumph; overnight success. For new work or business, can sometimes suggest foreign connections or international dealings.

Five of Wands > Knight of Pentacles > the World: Although it will take time and you may encounter obstacles and stiff competition, your diligence will finally bring assured success.

Six of Wands > the World: Prestigious accolades and awards of the highest order, possibly on the world stage.

The World > Ten of Wands: You may feel as though you have the weight of the world on your shoulders; the pressures of success, or success brings additional responsibilities.

The World > Four of Cups: An anticlimactic result once the buzz and adrenaline has died down. There may be a lack of appreciation of how good things are, but the suggestion is a lack of fulfilment despite success.

Knight of Cups > the World > Eight of Cups: Walking away from what appears to be an exceptional offer.

The World > Two of Pentacles: Maintaining the status quo and your position; reaching the top can be difficult but often requires careful manoeuvring to maintain it.

The World > Seven of Pentacles: International investments or payments.

Eight of Pentacles > the Emperor > the World > Knight of Wands: Suggests new work in a senior position (top of the tree), which can lead to relocation (possibly even international/emigration), or could involve plenty of foreign travel.

Ten of Swords > Wheel of Fortune > the World: From one extreme to another, and a blessing in disguise; what appears to be a disappointing ending opens the door for a wonderful opportunity to present itself and the results are better than you could have anticipated. The Ten of Swords and the World both show completion, from opposite ends of the scale.

Strength > Ace of Swords > the World: This triumph is hard-won through sheer persistence and determination over challenges and leads to everything coming up trumps.

The World > the Hermit > Temperance: Quiet and understated success, the simple enjoyment and appreciation of success with a moderate and balanced lifestyle brings harmony.

The Sun, the Moon, the Star, the World: Watch for this cosmic line-up of celestial bodies appearing anywhere in a larger spread, as it can represent material and spiritual integration, complete fulfilment of the inner and outer world. Harmonious aspects; "as above so below," heaven on earth, and being at one with the world; perfect alignment.

IV
Final Notes

The Probable Future

The Oxford dictionary interpretation for divination states: "The act of finding out and saying what will happen in the future." My own thoughts and conclusion to reading the future is that we're not treating the reading as a fatalistic outcome (one where the client has no control) but one based upon the potential and most likely outcome from the path the client is already travelling; events set in motion and the result of where past and present actions or choices are leading.

The future can often throw unanticipated curveballs, and whilst we may not be able to control everything that happens in our lives, we do have control over our response to any situation. Foreseeing a potential outcome provides us with the ability to make an informed decision by either continuing to follow the current course of action, or exploring options that could help find a better alternative. For the most part, much remains within our control through our own actions or inaction. As for those occasional incidents and external events that affect us where we feel we have no involvement or agency, we tend to frame these situations as fate, destiny, or chance.

The beauty of tarot is that it not only shows what may be coming down the track but also a client's mental or emotional side; the influence of their hopes, fears, and attitudes within a given situation; and where they have the power to create a shift. For most readers, the purpose of the reading is to make a positive difference in helping the client, not simply to provide an answer but to empower them through the information that comes to light.

Readings can serve as an early warning system. If the potential future isn't lining up as hoped, you can ask the client what their other options are and if they have a plan B to help them consider other possibilities. You could then explore other avenues that are available to them by asking a new question with a fresh spread to help discover other opportunities or different routes they could take that would be more successful.

Six Degrees of Separation

I'm sure some of the featured combinations made you wonder how realistic they could be, but people's lives are often surprising; and you never know who you may have sitting in front of you or their wider connections. Situations surrounding surveillance or gang activities, for example, seem to be more commonplace than they used to be, in broader terms. It's not as though someone rocks up for a reading looking like a movie stereotype straight off the set of a James Bond movie or *The Sopranos*—people can unwittingly or innocently get caught in the middle of situations through family or wider associations around them. It's best to always keep an open mind… truth is often stranger than fiction!

Breaking It Down: Reading Checklist Summary

Tarot combinations form part of the bigger picture as you work through a reading. Most of the time you'll see the connections, but if you're struggling to make sense of a spread, try going back to basics and breaking it down. Here's a quick summary checklist of things that may help:

1. Say your keywords in your mind as you lay down each card.

2. As a first impression, what is your automatic response to what's in front of you, how does it make you feel: good, bad, mixed, or indifferent?

3. When you say your keywords, do the cards flow together easily or do they seem choppy, disjointed, or contradictory? The pattern of the cards can sometimes reveal things quite literal in the landscape of possible outcomes: the flow of events as to how they would be experienced as the situation unfolds.

4. Go back and read the cards fully as a progression of events, one leading to the next, expanding on your keywords to the full meanings of the cards to reveal the story.

5. Look for common denominators and any repeating themes, such as:

   • Are there similar meanings to strengthen and reinforce an interpretation?

   • Which suits are present? Does one dominate, highlighting a theme?

   • Are there any multiple numbers?

   • If the pip cards (the numbered minor arcana) fall into a group of low or higher numbers, it can also reveal the progress on the journey, early days, midpoint, or nearing completion.

6. What is the trajectory as you move forwards: is the situation improving or worsening as you progress through the reading? Look for positive cards hampered by negative cards following or on either side and vice versa.

7. Absent cards can be telling. If you asked a question, which cards would you anticipate being present?

8. As a process of elimination, sometimes it can be illuminating to work backwardss. Look at the meaning of the final outcome card and go back to the beginning to see how the other cards led there. Hanged-Man thinking can provide a fresh perspective!

Endnote

Our journey with tarot is a constant work in progress drawn from fresh insights through our working experiences. Some of the perspectives I have presented may be useful, yet others you may find don't sit easily with you. As always, I encourage you to find your own personal language and interpretation for the cards that work well for you and provide good results. Many of the combinations I discovered in readings were initially jotted down afterwards as I found them interesting, but then became fixtures due to their reliability. Similarly, your personal notes can be constantly tweaked and updated as your own style finds form.

Mindful of my own early journey, within these pages I have tried to share as much as I can in the hope it might help alleviate some of the challenges you may encounter along the way. I encourage you to explore, adapt, and make your journey your own, and then spread your wings as you embark upon your tarot odyssey of wonder and discovery. As readers, we pass on the baton as we share our secrets in the hope that it is of benefit in helping others. If you should find sufficient value from my insights to carry them forwards into your own readings, then my task would be accomplished and complete. I wish you abundant blessings on your way!

Bibliography

Connolly, Eileen. *Tarot: A New Handbook for the Apprentice*. Wellingborough, UK: Aquarian Press, 1979, 1986.

———. *The Handbook for the Journeyman*. Wellingborough, UK: Aquarian Press, 1987, 1990.

DuQuette, Lon Milo. *Understanding Aleister Crowley's Thoth Tarot*. Newburyport, MA: Red Wheel/Weiser, 2003.

Ellershaw, Josephine. *Easy Tarot: Learn to Read the Cards Once and For All!* St. Paul, MN: Llewellyn Publications, 2007.

———. *Easy Tarot Reading: The Process Revealed in Ten True Readings*. Woodbury, MN: Llewellyn Publications, 2011.

Greer, Mary. *Tarot For Your Self, 2nd Edition*. Newburyport, MA: New Page Books, 2002.

Huson, Paul. *Mystical Origins of the Tarot: From Ancient Roots to Modern Usage*. Rochester, VT: Destiny Books, 2004.

Kaplan, Stuart R. *Tarot Cards for Fun and Fortune Telling: Illustrated Guide to the Spreading and Interpretation of the Popular 78-Card Tarot*. Stamford, CT: US Games Systems, 1970.

Moore, Barbara. *The Gilded Tarot Companion.* St. Paul, MN: Llewellyn Publications, 2005.

Pollack, Rachel. *Rachel Pollack's Tarot Wisdom: Spiritual Teachings and Deeper Meanings.* Woodbury, MN: Llewellyn Publications, 2008.

Waite, Arthur Edward. *The Pictorial Key to the Tarot.* Stamford, CT: US Games Systems, 2001. Originally published 1910 by William Rider & Son (London).

To Write to the Author

If you wish to contact the author or would like more information about this book, please write to the author in care of Llewellyn Worldwide Ltd. and we will forwards your request. Both the author and publisher appreciate hearing from you and learning of your enjoyment of this book and how it has helped you. Llewellyn Worldwide Ltd. cannot guarantee that every letter written to the author can be answered, but all will be forwardsed. Please write to:

Josephine Ellershaw
℅ Llewellyn Worldwide
2143 Wooddale Drive
Woodbury, MN 55125-2989
Please enclose a self-addressed stamped envelope
for reply, or $1.00 to cover costs. If outside the U.S.A., enclose an
international postal reply coupon.

Many of Llewellyn's authors have websites with additional information and resources. For more information, please visit our website at:
http://www.llewellyn.com

THE FOOL.